Talleyrand's Successor

Le Duc de Richelieu.

Né le 25 7bre 1766. Mort le 17 Mai 1822.

ARMAND-EMMANUEL DU PLESSIS
(Fifth Duc de Richelieu)

Talleyrand's Successor

Armand-Emmanuel du Plessis Duc de Richelieu 1766–1822

by

CYNTHIA COX

ARTHUR BARKER Ltd
LONDON 1959

MADE AND PRINTED IN GREAT BRITAIN BY
MORRISON AND GIBB LIMITED, LONDON AND EDINBURGH

CONTENTS

PROLOGUE 9

PART ONE. SOLDIER

I. ANCESTRAL BACKGROUND 13
II. EDUCATION OF AN HEIR 20
III. MARRIAGE 26
IV. GERMAN JOURNEY 30
V. BAPTISM OF FIRE 36
VI. FROM PILLAR TO POST 50

PART TWO. GOVERNOR-GENERAL

I. NEW-RUSSIA 63
II. ODESSA 69
III. THE FIELD WIDENS 75
IV. WARS AND EXCURSIONS 85
V. THE VALLEY OF THE SHADOW . . . 100

PART THREE. PRIME MINISTER

I. PRELUDE 113
II. THE HUNDRED DAYS 120
III. THE POLITICAL JUNGLE 133
IV. THE PEACE TREATY 142
V. LIBERATION OF THE TERRITORY . . . 152
VI. EXIT THE MINISTRY 166
VII. ESCAPE TO FREEDOM 174
VIII. RECAPTURED 185
IX. EUROPE IN TURMOIL 192
X. FINAL DEFEAT 203
XI. JOURNEY'S END 213

LIST OF ILLUSTRATIONS

ARMAND-EMMANUEL DU PLESSIS, FIFTH DUC DE
RICHELIEU, 1766–1822 . . *Frontispiece*

Facing page

LOUIS FRANCOIS ARMAND DU PLESSIS, THIRD DUC DE
RICHELIEU, MARSHAL OF FRANCE (PHOTOGRAPH
COPYRIGHT LES BEAUX ARTS) . . . 18

ODESSA IN THE NINETEENTH CENTURY . . . 73

TSAR ALEXANDER I (REPRODUCED BY GRACIOUS PER-
MISSION OF HER MAJESTY THE QUEEN) . . 92

CHARLES PHILIPPE, COMTE D'ARTOIS (MONSIEUR) . 117

LOUIS XVIII 126

THE MARQUISE DE MONTCALM (FROM A LITHOGRAPH
BY LEMERCIER). 134

ELIE, DUC DECAZES 170

ACKNOWLEDGMENTS

The portrait of Tsar Alexander I on p. 92 is from the Royal Collection at Windsor, and is reproduced by gracious permission of Her Majesty the Queen. Other illustrations are reproduced by kind permission of the Bibliothéque Nationale and the Trustees of the British Museum and of the Victoria and Albert Museum.

I would also like to record my appreciation of the helpful courtesy shown to me by M. Marcel Rieunier, Secretary-General of the Bibliothèque Nationale; by M. Maurice Piquard, Chief Librarian of the Bibliothèques de l'Université de Paris, and by the Librarian in charge of the Bibliothèque Victor Cousin in the Sorbonne.

CYNTHIA COX

PROLOGUE

THREE months had passed since the battle of Waterloo. H.M.S. *Northumberland* was well under way on her long voyage to the south Atlantic, carrying the disturber of Europe's peace to the island rock where it was hoped that he would at last be placed beyond the power of causing further upheaval.

But France was left to pay the reckoning. With her male population decimated by years of warfare and her economy disrupted, she found herself after the Hundred Days facing the exasperated European Powers whose Vienna peacemaking had been interrupted by the renewal of a war already waged for over twenty years. They were now clamouring for the punishment of France, even the dismemberment of her territory. Crisis at home was added to the grave perils threatening France from the outside. The parliamentary elections held in August had brought in a rabidly Royalist Chamber which was violently hostile to the moderate government in office, particularly to the two leaders of the cabinet: Talleyrand, the renegade aristocrat who had served every régime in turn, and Fouché the ex-regicide; an unseemly coalition stigmatised by Chateaubriand as " Vice supported on the arm of Crime." Talleyrand, moreover, was as much disliked by the Bourbons, who had never been able to believe him unconnected with the death of the Duc d'Enghien, as he was by the Tsar Alexander of Russia, who could not forgive him for his part in bringing France into the anti-Russian alliance of January 1815. In view of the militant hostility of the Chambers, Talleyrand himself was by no means unwilling to go into what he thought could be only a temporary retirement. He would thus leave to his successor the odium of negotiating the peace treaty, which he well realised was bound to be a hard

9

one. Having decided to make a strategic withdrawal from office, he did not hesitate to describe the document setting forth the Allies' terms as " perhaps even more insolent in its form than in the iniquitous demands it contained."

A new pilot was now urgently needed to guide the French ship of state through the dangerous shoals ahead, a man of distinction but above all of integrity, whose name—unlike that of Talleyrand—would have no unfortunate associations with the past. It was not easy to find such a man, after all the storm and stress of the previous quarter century. Yet in the opinion of both Louis XVIII and the Tsar Alexander, there was one, a man of the highest integrity and bearer of a great name, who was eminently suited to fill this role. To him Count Molé was to write imploringly : " In this universal shipwreck of reputations and good names, yours alone has remained unsullied. Who else but you can reassure Europe over France and France over herself ? " He had been away from France for twenty-four years, making his career in Russia ; whence Talleyrand's malicious quip about his being an excellent choice since he was the man with the best knowledge of the Crimea. He was, however, a personal friend of the Tsar Alexander, the most powerful sovereign in the European alliance, whom he had served with distinction for a number of years. France herself was now in dire need of such devoted service, and fortunate circumstance had produced the man who seemed most fitted to give it : Armand-Emmanuel du Plessis, Duc de Richelieu.

PART ONE

SOLDIER

CHAPTER I

ANCESTRAL BACKGROUND

His family came originally from Poitou. In the rugged north-
eastern corner where the river Creuse winds it way down
from the *massif central* towards the Loire, the granite rocks
pile up into high walls towering above the river. Here in
the early Middle Ages the duke's ancestors had built a stronghold on top of the cliffs. A fortified mound surrounded by
palisades and known as a *plessis*, it was to give its name to the
family who built it. In this countryside, wild and remote in
those early times, the du Plessis led a life of marauding
violence neither better nor worse than that of the majority of
their contemporaries. But towards the end of the fifteenth
century, the marriage of a son of the younger branch of the
family with Perrine Clérembault brought them connections
with the Court. For Perrine's brother Louis was major-domo
to Charles VII's queen, Marie of Anjou, and when Louis died
childless in 1490, he left to his nephew François du Plessis
practically all his fortune and estate, including that of
Richelieu, situated just inside the boundaries of Touraine.
The castle of Richelieu at that period was a typical feudal
stronghold which must have been as entrancing to the eye
as many of those still to be found to-day scattered about
Touraine. Built during the Hundred Years' War on an island
in the river Mable, it stood surrounded by a moat, its eight
towers crowned with conical caps and its main roof sur-
mounted by the strange riot of turrets and chimneys often to
be found in buildings dating to the early years of the French
Renaissance.

The inheritance of this estate by François du Plessis, and
the career at Court which his uncle's influence opened to him,

proved to be a turning point in the fortunes of the family. For while the elder branch continued to remain in provincial obscurity, the descendants of François, who thereafter took the name of du Plessis de Richelieu, soon began to make their mark in the history of France, strengthening their position by marriages with powerful families.   Thus in 1542, Louis du Plessis married into the great family of Rochechouart, and the son of this marriage, another François, was made Grand Provost of France for his loyal services to the last Valois king, Henri III.   He continued to hold the same office under Henri IV until carried off suddenly by a fever in 1590 at the early age of forty-two.   He had married Suzanne de la Porte, the daughter of a famous advocate, and his widow was left with five young children to bring up on the most slender resources. For so far was the Richelieu family from being affluent at this time that in order to pay the Grand Provost's funeral expenses it was found necessary to pawn his collar of the Order of the Holy Ghost which had been conferred on him by his King. His mother, Françoise de Rochechouart, a woman of militant disposition and consumed with family pride, considered that her son had married beneath him.   Life cannot therefore have been particularly pleasant for his widow, shut up with her mother-in-law in the castle of Richelieu, from which it was rarely possible to stir outside owing to the disturbed condition of the countryside.   For the Wars of Religion, in which the du Plessis had taken their part as followers of the Guises, had raged with particular ferocity in the country between Tours and Poitiers, and the roads were still infested with gangs of disbanded soldiers.   It was thus under no easy circumstances that the quiet, sensible woman who was the widow of François du Plessis, Lord of Richelieu, brought up her five children, of whom the youngest, Armand Jean, was destined to become the great Cardinal.

Having been created a peer of France and first Duc de Richelieu by his grateful king in 1631, the Cardinal obviously considered it necessary to justify the new importance of the family domain.   He therefore began to acquire other adjoining properties, including that of Chinon whose castle on the hill-top above the river Vienne had been the scene of many notable events during the Middle Ages. At Richelieu, he caused the King's architect, Jacques le Mercier, who was building for him in Paris the Palais Cardinal (later to be the Palais Royal), and reconstructing the Sorbonne, to prepare designs for a palatial new residence and town. François du Plessis had already begun to rebuild the old feudal fortress. His son now had the last remains of it demolished and in its place arose a splendid building set in extensive gardens and parkland, whose surrounding walls extended for nearly eight miles. The Secretary of State, Bouthillier, writing of it in May 1625, described it as " the most beautiful great mansion in Europe, only excepting Fontainebleau." (The splendour of Versailles, as yet no more than a royal hunting-lodge, still lay in the future.) La Grande Mademoiselle, who visited the château of Richelieu as a child, considered that such magnificence was only to be expected, " since it was the work of the most ambitious and most ostentatious man in the world." In order to ensure the pre-eminence of his own château, the Cardinal did not hesitate to eliminate possible competition by pulling down other structures on neighbouring properties that he bought. Soon the interior of his building became a treasure-house of painting and sculpture, for like other prominent people of the day he sent agents all over Italy to search for and buy works of art.

The little hamlet of Richelieu was also transformed under the hand of Le Mercier, blossoming forth in 1631 as a small town enclosed by high walls, containing magnificent private houses, a college, and a fine church. But the houses were in truth more suited to the capital's Faubourg St. Germain than to a small provincial town which in spite of all the Cardinal's efforts never became really flourishing. For the country round it was only poor and sterile marshland ; while the little town suffered the further grave disadvantage of being a number of miles from any main waterway or highroad. La Fontaine expressed satiric wonder that the Cardinal, who could do everything, had not caused either the Loire or the main high way to Bordeaux to be brought to Richelieu !

The Cardinal, however, did not live to see the completion of his architectural works, and at his death his property and ducal title passed to Armand-Jean de Vignerot, the grandson of his sister Françoise. The boy's father had been an incorrigible spendthrift whom even his imperious uncle's severe lectures had not availed to cure, and he was therefore passed over in the Cardinal's will. The second Duc de Richelieu seems to have left no particular claim to fame behind him, unless through the fact that he lived to what was then the remarkable age of eighty-six—though even this achievement was surpassed by the ninety-two-year life span of his son.

Louis-François-Armand, third Duc de Richelieu, one of the most notorious figures of the age of Louis XV, was described by Voltaire as the Alcibiades of France. Saint Simon wrote of him that at the age of sixteen he was " both in mind and body the most delightful little person imaginable. His father had presented him at Court, where Mme de Maintenon, an old friend of M. de Richelieu, adopted him as a son, and consequently everyone, from the King and the Duchesse de Bourgogne downward, spoiled him. He knew how to display such elegance and to comport himself with so much wit, freedom and politeness that he soon became the idol of the Court." The result of all this adulation, however, may be seen from the comments made in 1719 by the Princess Palatine : " He is small and beautifully made, graceful and not lacking in wit. But his insolence is unequalled, and he is the worst of all spoiled children." The opening of the new reign found him the acknowledged leader of the most intrepid young sparks in the corrupt court of the Orleans Regency, and he was soon in the Bastille, where he was to be lodged on three occasions during his early career, the first of these being the consequence of his having compromised the reputation of the Duchesse de Bourgogne, wife of the heir to the throne. However, his period of seclusion was most edifyingly employed on that occasion in the improvement of his classical education, and he produced a translation of Virgil which was later published by his tutor. His wit and his imperturbable audacity brought him into great favour with the Regent, as later with the young King, who found Richelieu's society a valuable antidote to that devastating sense of boredom which was already beginning to afflict His Majesty. Yet Louis XV did not always follow his friend's indications as to where he should bestow his favours, and Richelieu's influence suffered some degree of eclipse during the reign of Mme de Pompadour, whom all his hostility and malice could not avail to dislodge from her position; his efforts to this end merely producing from his royal crony a pointed enquiry as to how many times he had been in the Bastille. Yet when the Pompadour, goaded beyond endurance, suggested that her tormentor should be excluded from the gatherings of their little circle, the King only laughed and said that it would be quite useless attempting to do so, since if Richelieu were to be put out of the door, he would undoubtedly come back down the chimney.

There were, however, other aspects of the third duke's character which reveal some of the better qualities which he was to pass on to his grandson. When he was made Governor of Languedoc, for instance, he took his duties with sufficient seriousness to go and live there, which was more than most of his predecessors had troubled to do. Nor would he tolerate persecution of the Huguenots in his province by the bishops, seeing clearly enough that it was not in the interests of the State that this industrious section of the community should be driven to emigrate abroad. On the battlefield he was fearless, yet cool and resourceful. After his successful campaign in Italy during the War of the Austrian Succession, he was made a Marshal of France, and he led the French force which seized Minorca under the eyes of the British fleet commanded by the luckless Admiral Byng.

But the Marshal's entire life was spent in a state of continual financial difficulty, owing to his fantastic extravagance, of which a notable instance was his entry into Vienna as French Ambassador in 1725. On that occasion he made his appearance in the city escorted by no less than seventy-five carriages drawn by horses wearing silver shoes, so designed that the animals shed them in the streets as they went along. The carriages were accompanied by an army of running foot-men in splendid livery, while Richelieu himself, in full panoply of peer's robes, rode in an ornate coach decorated with symbolic figures. Certainly this splendour was as much for political as for personal ends, nor was Richelieu the only French ambassador to make a resplendent entry into a foreign capital. When the Marquis de Vérac arrived in St. Petersburg in 1779, he made his entry in a sumptuous glass coach whose body, lined with blue velvet interwoven with silver threads, was supported at its corners by four large silver figures. But on each occasion, the ambassadors spent their own money lavishly on their displays, and in Richelieu's case his continual heavy gambling did nothing to repair his fortune. He had few scruples about his means of replenishing it, however. During the last twelve months of his military career, at the beginning of the Seven Years' War, his attention was concentrated on the collection of loot rather than on the duties of his command, and his shameless behaviour in Westphalia caused even his own troops to nickname him " The Old Marauder."

His vitality up to the end of his life was remarkable. At eighty, he was still the very mirror of fashion : Voltaire unkindly described him as an " old doll," but that was when their lifelong friendship was imperilled by Voltaire's inability to recover interest on a loan which he had been rash enough to make to the incorrigible Marshal. At eighty-two, the old duke was seen mounting his horse " like a young soldier performing his exercises," and when the Archbishop of Paris invited him to dine at Conflans, he astonished his host by arriving on horseback and departing afterwards at a gallop. A few months later, he was to be seen at Versailles dancing a minuet at a state ball with the zest of a young courtier, while at the age of eighty-four he blithely embarked on his third matrimonial venture.

Richelieu's first marriage, to Anne Catherine de Noailles,

LOUIS FRANÇOIS ARMAND DU PLESSIS
(Third Duc de Richelieu, Marshal of France)

who was several years older than himself, had been a family arrangement in which his personal feelings were scarcely considered. It was indeed a marriage in little more than name, and ribald tongues were soon saying that Richelieu, like Cæsar, was the husband of every woman except his own wife. The marriage lasted for less than six years, however, for Anne Catherine died in 1716, and it was eighteen years before Richelieu married again. His second marriage to Marie Elizabeth Sophie de Lorraine, second daughter of the Prince de Guise, was not only one of social advantage (though the haughty Guises considered it to be a *mésalliance*) but was also one of real affection. In fact Richelieu was so much in love with his wife that he startled the Court by remaining faithful to her for a whole six months after his marriage. This second marriage resulted in the birth of two children, one of whom, as Duc de Fronsac, became his heir. Fronsac seems to have been an ineffective person who inherited his father's worst failings without either the Marshal's ability or charm. He appears indeed to have been overshadowed all his life by his remarkable parent, though such honours and titles as he received were actually due to that parent's influence ; he was, for instance, made colonel of the Septimanie Regiment at the mature age of seven. He grew up to become a prominent member of the band of scatterbrained young rakes who gathered round their kindred spirit, the Comte d'Artois, youngest brother of Louis XVI. Fronsac was in fact one of the ringleaders in their campaign for the performance of Beaumarchais's *Le Mariage de Figaro*, at first forbidden even by the easygoing King, who declared that its author mocked at everything which ought to be respected in a government. In due course, however, a suitable match was arranged for Richelieu's heir, and in 1764 he was married to Adelaide-Gabrielle, a daughter of the Marquis de Hautefort by his second wife. Two years later, on the 25th September 1766, the Duchesse de Fronsac gave birth in Paris to a son who received the names of Armand-Emmanuel Sophie Septimanie du Plessis, and the title of Comte de Chinon.

CHAPTER II

EDUCATION OF AN HEIR

THE young Duchesse de Fronsac did not live very long after the birth of her son. In the following year, she died of "a chest complaint," leaving the infant Armand Emmanuel virtually an orphan, since his father took little interest in him—not that it was ever the habit of eighteenth-century French nobles to take any interest in their children until they became old enough for the arrangement of suitable marriage alliances. The duchess's two sisters, however, took charge of the child, and what he lacked in paternal affection was more than made up to him by his grandfather. For the Marshal Duc de Richelieu, though he had had scant sympathy or patience with his son, doted upon his grandson who, he predicted, would have his good qualities without having his defects.

Fortunately, however, it was not left to the Marshal to preside over his grandson's education, His own son had not been a conspicuous example of his success in this direction, and indeed something of his ideas and methods may be gauged from an anecdote which has been related by his grandson. One day when the boy was eight years old and had entered his grandfather's room to wish him good morning, the duke, who had had a very successful evening's play with the King the night before, tossed the child a purse containing forty louis,[1] 'for his pocket money.' A fortnight later, on a similar occasion, the old duke observed to his grandson : " I must replenish your purse ; it must be empty." " Oh, no, grandpapa," replied the child, " I still have the forty louis you gave me." Whereupon the duke opened his window and threw the

---

[1] The *louis*, a gold coin equivalent in value to the English guinea, was in use from the time of Louis XIII up to the Revolution.

purse out to a beggar who was passing by, calling out to him :
" Here, my good man, take these forty louis that my grandson
has not known how to spend in a fortnight." It is not perhaps
surprising if the feminine members of the Richelieu family
should have closed their ranks in a protective circle round the
one and only heir, to ensure that he should have a less disastrous upbringing than his father and grandfather. His
paternal aunt, the Comtesse d'Egmont, combined with his
great-aunt, the Duchesse d'Aiguillon to impress this necessity
upon the Duc de Fronsac, and they urged that as soon as the
boy became old enough he should be placed under the care of
the Abbé Labdan, a most worthy and admirable man who subsequently became tutor to the ill-fated Duc d'Enghien. So
far, indeed, was the end held to justify the means in this vital
cause that Mme d'Egmont did not hesitate to appeal to the
actress Sophie Arnould to exert her influence, since Fronsac
was known to be at that time in the beatific state of being
unable to refuse her anything.

As a result of the combined efforts of all these ladies, the
young Comte de Chinon was placed under the care of the Abbé
Labdan. In the following year, at the age of eight, he entered
the Collège du Plessis, the family foundation which had been
restored and reinvigorated by the great Cardinal, and which
was renowned not only for the excellence of its educational
methods but also for the strictness of its discipline. Since it
soon became apparent that the Comte de Chinon had inherited
the quick intelligence of his grandfather, he was to prove an
apt pupil.

It was the custom in those days for French nobles to
arrange marriages for their children while they were still at
schools or convents. The Prince de Poix was married at
fifteen to a bride of seventeen ; which circumstance, as he was
later to remark ingenuously in his memoirs, " did much harm
to my education, which was never finished." When the heir
of the Duc de Doudeauville was fetched out of school at the
age of fourteen to be married, the principal of the establishment demurred as the boy was at the time in detention ; but

we are told that he withdrew his objections instantly on hear-
ing that the young Vicomte was leaving school to be married.
Obviously the future of the Duc de Richelieu's heir could be
no less a matter of anxious concern to his family, and when
Chinon had reached the age of æfteen, his great-aunt Mme de
Beringhau arranged for him a marriage with Rosalie, one of
the three daughters of Comte Louis-Roger de Rochechouart.
Almost directly afterwards, in August 1782, the boy was sent
off with his tutor on a three-year tour of Europe, the Grand
Tour which was considered such an indispensable finish to the
education of a young eighteenth-century nobleman.   In this
case, it may well have laid the foundations of the insatiable
delight in travel and in seeing new places which was to remain
characteristic of Chinon throughout his life.

The two travellers set off for Italy, spending some time on
the way in Geneva, whence the Abbé Labdan wrote that they
were busy learning Italian ; from the moment they set foot in
Italy, he said, they would be speaking no more French, for he
wished to " give M. de Chinon a strong enough dose of Italian
to last him the rest of his life."   The journey into Italy over
the Simplon Pass must have been, to say the least, heavy going
in 1782, for the highroad over the pass had yet to be made by
Napoleon ; but they crossed the mountains without mishap
and eventually reached Florence.   Here Prince Charles Edward
was still living under the name of the Count of Albany.   The
Marshal Duc de Richelieu had been on the point of leading a
French expedition to the aid of the Young Pretender in 1745 ;
when it was seen, however, that the rising was not progressing
according to plan, enthusiasm had rapidly cooled in Paris.   But
the Prince now received the Marshal's grandson graciously,
and Chinon had some interesting conversation with him,
particularly about the events leading up to the revolution of
1688.   The Prince seems to have expressed himself with remarkable candour about the obstinacy and bigotry of his own
grandfather who, he declared, had shown no respect for an
enlightened age.   After remaining for some while in Florence,
Chinon and his tutor then resumed their tour of Italy ; finally,

recrossing the Alps into Austria, they took the road to Vienna.

Since the death of Maria Theresa two years earlier, her son Joseph II was now reigning alone. Chinon had already been presented to him as a child when the Austrian monarch, travelling in Europe under the name of Count von Falkenstein, had come to Paris to visit his sister Marie Antoinette. Now that they met again, Chinon's quiet modesty and his aptitude for languages (he already spoke German, English and Italian, unusual accomplishments for a French noble) made a very favourable impression on both the Emperor and on his Chancellor Kaunitz, as also on the Prince de Ligne, one of the most distinguished men of the day. With the Prince's son Charles, Chinon was to form a close friendship.

If the Court of Vienna took the young Comte de Chinon to its heart, he for his part was certainly much attracted by Vienna. The gay, pleasure-loving city and musical capital of Europe was now under the rule of a young emperor nourished on the enlightened rationalism of the French philosophers. The whole atmosphere of the Austrian capital made a strong appeal to the lively intelligence of the youth who was making his first acquaintance with the life of other European countries. There were, too, very potent personal reasons for Chinon's attachment to the city : " It is there," he was to say in later life, " that I spent my best years ; it is there that I had those first love affairs which leave an indelible impression on the heart." Chinon's affection for Vienna was to remain with him throughout his life, and during all the vicissitudes of the years to come he never missed an opportunity of revisiting the city.

The Comte de Langeron, a lifelong friend from Vienna days, gives an interesting portrait of Chinon, " whose astonishing resemblance to his grandfather struck all those who had known the Marshal in his youth. He was tall, lanky, very thin, a little bent. At the age of fifteen his face was charming, and it remained pleasing to the end of his life. Its chief ornament was a pair of large dark eyes full of fire, which gave his face an expression both of wit and piquancy. He was of very dark complexion, with curly and intensely black hair, which turned grey very early." Mme de Boigne, a less friendly witness, said of him that he was very short sighted ; this was certainly true, for in later life when he went about on social occasions he would ask those with him to tell him if there were any people present to whom he particularly ought to bow, that he might not appear discourteous through omitting to do so. When he was in Odessa, he always made a point of bowing when passing the large balcony in the front of the club, though he was too short sighted to see whether or not anyone was actually there, and sometimes there happened to be nobody upon it.

With regard to his personality, Langeron says that from his youth Chinon showed an austerity of character and a certain stiffness astonishing in so young a man ; that he was not made for the frivolous society of his time and seemed out of place in it ; but that his fine qualities were so apparent that his contemporaries, although they might not always find him congenial, could not help respecting him. Much of this side of his character was probably due to his training in the austere surroundings of the Collège du Plessis. There, too, was cultivated in a naturally active brain the keen desire for knowledge which never left him throughout his life and which was greatly assisted by his remarkably good memory and his capacity for absorbing instruction of all kinds. Not only had he a well-stocked mind, but he had also the ability to express himself with great fluency on paper, in writing that was neat, compact and small. Langeron says that he was capable of writing several pages upon the most abstract subjects without needing to alter a single word of what he had written ; that his style, like his conversation, was clear, concise and full of ideas. Decazes, who was to be his colleague for several years in later life, said exactly the same of him. His stiffness in society undoubtedly sprang from shyness, which his Spartan upbringing could certainly have done nothing to eradicate. Langeron tells us that he was timid and embarrassed in the presence of women—a remarkable trait in a Richelieu—but that in small gatherings of people whom he knew really well and liked, he could be gay even to the point of being boisterous. The arrival in the gathering of anyone less well known, however, would cause him at once to retire again into his shell. Nor did he always find it easy to come out of it in the presence even of those whom he knew really well. His relations with his two half-sisters, Mmes de Montcalm and de Jumilhac, were always of a most affectionate nature ; yet when in later life he returned to France after many years' absence, even Mme de Montcalm, with whom he had maintained an intimate correspondence, had to confess that she found him at first a little intimidating. This seems chiefly to have been on account of a certain abruptness of manner, and an outspoken directness which was the reflection of his fundamental honesty of character. Sensitive and very highly strung, he suffered much from migraine during the harassing days of his later career. Hence he tended always to take the most despondent view of difficulties which confronted him—largely through underrating his own capacity to deal with them. Although actually possessing great reserves of physical energy and endurance, yet in times of intense mental stress he was capable of worrying himself into a state of complete collapse—as in the first great crisis of his life which was now about to confront him.

CHAPTER III

MARRIAGE

DURING the three years of his absence abroad, Chinon had
been receiving constant letters from his future wife, written
with a grace and wit which charmed him and augured well
for the future.   At his request, she had also sent him her
portrait—which in the light of subsequent events must have
been a very flattering one.   Thus when the time came for him
to return and claim his bride, he arrived home, a handsome
youth of eighteen, in a state of happy anticipation.

But unfortunately nobody had thought it necessary to
prepare him for the shock which awaited him.   His young
wife had developed some form of spinal trouble which had
turned her into a hunchback completely deformed both back
and front—" as hump-backed as Punchinello " in the words
of her cousin Léon de Rochechouart.   Even without such a
tragic degree of deformity, poor Rosalie de Rochechouart,
unusually short of stature with a large nose and inordinately
long arms, could scarcely have laid claim to physical beauty ;
but in any case such details were considered quite irrelevant
in the arrangement of a match so desirable on other grounds.
According to Mme de Boigne, when Chinon arrived in Paris
and hurried eagerly to the Hôtel de Richelieu (which with its
gardens stood upon the site partly occupied to-day by the
Gare St. Lazare), he was received by his father and grandfather, who brought forward and presented to him as his life's
companion " a little stooping hump-backed monster."   The
unhappy youth is said to have taken one look at his bride,
recoiled three steps backward and fainted.   He was carried in
a state of collapse to his room, from which he refused to
emerge ; but presently he wrote to his relatives that he felt

quite unable to consummate the marriage. He then ordered post-horses in order to set forth on his travels again. Such at any rate was the tale which went the round of the Paris *salons*; it would lose nothing in the telling. The marriage ceremony certainly took place, but it is equally certain that on coming out of church, the bridegroom at once set off alone to return to Vienna, the scene of so many pleasant memories.

Not the least tragic aspect of the affair was that beneath her appallingly misshapen exterior, the poor bride seems to have possessed an unusually generous and gentle disposition. As much attracted by the sight of her young husband as he was repelled by the sight of her, she did her best to calm down the storm which arose between the two families after the bridegroom's precipitate flight, and even offered to support any attempt he might choose to make to have the marriage annulled. But it was not in Chinon's make-up to go back upon his word; moreover, when the first shock had worn off, he was touched by her attitude—and perhaps stung by remorse for his own part in the affair. After his departure for Vienna, the newly made Comtesse de Chinon, unable to face the pitiless gossip of Paris, withdrew to Courteilles in the department of Eure-et-Loir near Chartres. There she lived quietly with her parents and grandmother on the fine estate in the valley of the Avre which had come into her family on the death of her maternal grandfather, the Marquis de Courteilles, in the château which had been constructed about 1773 by the famous architect Carpentier, the builder of the Palais Bourbon. Mme de Boigne says of her that " she was the good genius of the whole Richelieu family. Far from showing resentment (towards her husband), she constantly manifested her disinterested friendship by the most delicate attentions, and gave no sign that she was ever animated by any keener sentiment than friendship." The Abbé Nicolle, speaking of her in later years, said that in addition to her qualities of disposition she possessed a delicate wit, was very well informed and a delightful conversationalist, so that one found at Courteilles many of the pleasures of Parisian society. This was no doubt

true, but, on the other hand, when the Tsar visited Paris at
the time of the Restoration and the Duchesse de Richelieu, as
she was then, was received by him in audience, the Russian
sovereign, who was far from being unappreciative of the
opposite sex, could not resist confiding afterwards to Léon
de Rochechouart : " Now I understand the Duc de Richelieu's
behaviour towards his wife. My dear fellow, how ugly and
frightful looking she is ! I am sure she has much wit and
great qualities, but at twenty years of age it would have
needed superhuman courage to overlook such ugliness."

The Comte de Chinon's absence abroad after his marriage
cannot have lasted very long, however, for in 1785 the Marshal
Duc de Richelieu was at last conquered by *anno Domini* and
found himself at the age of eighty-nine obliged to relinquish
the post of First Gentleman of the Bedchamber which he had
held in the King's household for no less than forty-four years.
As Fronsac, though not yet fifty, was already too decrepit to
take his father's place, the old duke's mantle fell upon his
grandson, who found himself at the early age of nineteen
doomed to be a daily participant in the wearisome ceremonial
of the royal *lever* and *coucher*. What was worse, the office
entailed his being in constant attendance at Versailles, among
the young courtiers with whom he had nothing in common
save only his love for the profession of arms. He was now a
junior officer in the Queen's Regiment of Dragoons and was
longing for the opportunity of seeing some active service. At
that time the only part of Europe where there was any chance
of gratifying such a wish was in Russia, which under the rule
of Catherine the Great was steadily pursuing a policy of
expansion at the expense of the Ottoman Empire. Russia had
thus become a magnet for many restless young nobles anxious
for military glory, especially those who had already fought in
the American War of Independence, and when war actually
broke out between Russia and Turkey in 1787, Chinon applied
for leave of absence to serve with the Russian army. Roger
de Damas had already departed in secret to the war while on
leave, and Langeron, a veteran of the American war at fifteen,

also offered his sword to the Empress Catherine, who announced on seeing his letter that " Every man of good birth and honour who wishes to enter my army will be received in it."   But the heir of the house of Richelieu was not accorded permission to go ; he had to find consolation in a tour of duty with his regiment, after which he contrived to pay another visit to Vienna.   He was still there in August 1788 when the old Duc de Richelieu died—less than twelve months before the first definitive rumblings of the storm which was to sweep away " the old doll's " world for ever.   His son now assumed the title, and his grandson returned to France as Duc de Fronsac.

CHAPTER IV

GERMAN JOURNEY

As spring came to 1789, so too did food riots. Aftermath of the previous year's disastrous harvest, they were the lightning on the horizon before the approaching storm which was to break in July. Although by the autumn the full fury of the outburst had for the time being died down again in Paris to a low rumble of discontent, under the goad of continued economic stress it rose once more to storm pitch at the beginning of October when the mob marched out to Versailles.

The new Duc de Fronsac, by now a captain in the Esterhazy Regiment of Hussars as well as First Gentleman of the Bedchamber, was at the time in Paris. Deciding that he must at all costs try to reach Versailles ahead of the populace in order to warn the royal family, he disguised himself in old clothes as one of the crowd and mingling with them, set out on foot. But the Route de Sèvres was already so blocked that he soon realised the impossibility of arriving in time by that road, and he turned off towards Meudon, making his way through the woods. He reached Versailles at the very moment when the mob was converging on the château, and hurrying straight to the Queen persuaded her to move for safety into the King's apartments. In his soldier's ardour, Fronsac would have had the King put himself at the head of his troops and retire to Rambouillet; but such heroic measures were not in the nature of poor Louis XVI, who was to remain to the end what he had always been : the inert victim of circumstances. So the royal family dutifully returned to Paris to become virtually prisoners in the Tuileries, and the fateful year 1789 slipped into 1790.

In April of that year, the Duchesse de Fronsac lost one of her sisters. It was then, she declared, that her husband showed her " all the kindness and sensitive feeling of his heart." It is clear that although they were never to live together as husband and wife, during the six years which had passed since the disastrous beginning of their marriage their relationship had settled down into a kindly mutual understanding which was to endure for the rest of their lives. Fronsac remained at his wife's side until the end of that summer. He then went to rejoin his regiment, which was in garrison at Sedan, and shortly afterwards was charged with the mission of revisiting Vienna in order to sound the attitude of Joseph II towards the recent happenings in France. Unfortunately, just as he was about to start on his journey, the Emperor Joseph died. Fronsac none the less set out for Germany, ostensibly in order to attend the coronation of the new emperor at Frankfort ; his real purpose, however, was to gather information about the attitude of the German princes towards the revolution in France.

He started from Sedan on the 2nd September, making for Luxembourg through the Ardennes. The country through which he travelled was of course in those days very wild ; he notes in his journal, rather surprisingly, that the Ardennes were "ugly" and arid. But as we shall see, his idea of beautiful country was a region well covered with prosperous villages and set in the midst of intensively cultivated land—not perhaps the ideal of scenic beauty in the overcrowded twentieth century, but typical of the age of the Physiocrats. Thus, though unmoved by the purely scenic grandeur of the Ardennes, Fronsac found the serene, well-populated valley of Liège "superb." At ten miles beyond Liège he came to the first Austrian post. On discovery of his identity, he was allowed to pass freely, and continued on his way to Aix-la-Chapelle, which had already become an asylum for refugees from the revolutionary upheavals of both France and the Low Countries. From Aix, he continued via Bonn to the Palatinate, in order to visit his colonel the Prince de Salm. He found the

forty miles from Aix to Bonn enjoyable on account of the
smiling countryside—so different, he cannot resist pointing
out, from the "savage" Ardennes—and the Rhine at Bonn was
imposing. From Bonn he went on to Coblentz, along the left
bank of the Rhine through enchanting scenery, the road wind-
ing among vineyards, usually with fine views of both sides of
the river. Beyond Coblentz he entered the Palatinate by a
"detestable road" and spent the rest of the month making his
way along by easy stages, paying calls of several days at a time
on various old friends, beginning with his colonel. Finally,
on the 27th September, he arrived at Frankfort, where he
joined forces with the Vicomte de Caraman, who was already
there. Frankfort was now a hive of activity preparing for all
the complicated ceremonial attendant on the coronation of a
new emperor. Fronsac's account is of particular interest,
since in a little over fifteen years from that time the Holy
Roman Empire would have ceased to exist, swept away for
ever by the iconoclastic hand of Napoleon.

The elective Diet had already been assembled since July,
each elector sending one, two or even three ambassadors. The
remarkable thing about it, observes Fronsac, was the almost
general ineffectiveness of all these gentlemen ; not, he hastens
to add, that he presumes to set himself up as a judge of such
matters ; he is merely reporting the general opinion of others.
The only exceptions to this melancholy rule were the Ambassador of Trèves, the Saxon Minister and the Prussian
Minister, Count von Goertz. The latter, subtle and very
witty, accustomed to handling important issues in the thorny
atmosphere of St. Petersburg, and combining with his political
acumen a great charm of manner, led the Diet exactly where
he wished it to go. When all the preliminary business had
been settled, the three ecclesiastical electors arrived in a truly
oriental display of magnificence. The Elector of Mainz, whose
pride, says Fronsac, was in inverse ratio to his birth, distinguished himself by the vast retinue of attendants which he
brought with him : no less than 1480 persons, including a
certain Fräulein von Gudenhofen, newly made a countess

for the occasion, and who fulfilled the functions of first
minister !

On the 30th September, the actual day of the election, the
ecclesiastical electors, together with the ambassadors, went in
full procession of carriages and retinue to the Town Hall.
There they mounted on horseback and in order according to
the rank they held in the Empire, they proceeded to the
church of St. Bartholemew, where Leopold was solemnly
acclaimed as the new emperor. The procession then returned
in the same order to the Town Hall. On the way, the Elector
of Cologne, a very popular prince who believed in the late
Emperor's principle that the ruler should be accessible to the
least of his subjects, caused a mild sensation by his unheard-of
behaviour in taking off his electoral cap and saluting the
populace with it cheerfully to right and to left. The Archbishop of Olmütz thereupon felt impelled to do likewise; but his
efforts were far from being received with the same enthusiasm.

The new emperor was not actually due to arrive until the
beginning of October, but meanwhile the concourse in
Frankfort increased, as a swarm of petty princes, counts and
barons of the Empire flocked into the city. Fronsac was not
impressed with these luminaries. Many of them, he says,
reigned over no more than a couple of villages, and in most
cases the number of quadrupeds in their domains greatly
exceeded the number of their subjects. It would be difficult
to find, he adds tartly, a gathering of more uncouth, more
mediocre and more insignificant persons than these rulers,
among whom were included the greater part of the hereditary
princes. He does not mention, and probably did not even
notice in such an assembly, the presence of a young Rhineland
nobleman of seventeen who was acting as Master of Ceremonies to the Order of Catholic Imperial Counts of Westphalia. The name of Clement von Metternich would have
meant little to Fronsac at that time ; he was no doubt much
more interested in the feminine portion of the gathering. This
he evidently did not find so displeasing, since he writes approv-
ingly of the great ball given by the Archbishop of Olmütz at

T.S.—3

which, among the several hundred women present, he notes
" a great number " very pretty and very well turned out·

On the 9th October, the Emperor, who had halted a while
at Aschaffenburg, approached to within a mile of Frankfort,
where he was received with great pomp by all the electors and
ambassadors, his arrival being announced by a salvo of 300
guns. Further salvoes announced the start of the procession,
and finally the actual entry of the Emperor into the town.
Each elector or ambassador was preceded by a hundred
carriages drawn by six horses each, accompanied by a large
retinue of liveried attendants. The Emperor's carriage, in
which he sat alone, was followed by his mounted guard, after
which came that of each of the three ecclesiastical electors.
The whole procession was terminated by the strange sight of
a squadron of yellow-clad postillions, armed with their cornets
and post whips. This odd and somewhat comic contrast of
magnificence and simplicity was an integral part of the
etiquette attaching to the ceremony. The huge procession
then made its way through the town, gathering around it an
ever-increasing multitude of people, to the church of St.
Bartholemew. Here the Emperor took the oath to maintain the constitution. He was then officially proclaimed by
the Elector of Mainz, to the shattering accompaniment of
trumpets, timbals, more salvoes of artillery, all the church
bells of the town, and the applause of the multitude. Fronsac's
comment, however, is that the magnificence of the proceedings
was considerably dimmed by its lack of order. But he gives
one or two interesting details of some of the strange ceremonies which occurred during the return of the procession
through the town. The Grand Marshal, for instance, was
obliged to jump on horseback into an immense heap of oats,
gather up a golden measure full and present it to the Emperor.
The Chief Carver had likewise to present the Emperor with a
slice of meat from an ox which was being roasted whole in a
specially built wooden shelter. This having been done, the
shelter collapsed and both the ox and the oats became the per-
quisites of the multitude, who not only disposed of both with

remarkable speed and ability but also gathered up the carpet upon which the Emperor had walked from the church to the Town Hall.

The nights following the coronation passed in a succession of balls, assemblies and suppers. In the course of several such evenings, Fronsac met a number of people who were able to supply him with some of the information he had come to seek. The German princes, it appeared, were really concerned only with obtaining compensation for the rights which some of their number had lost in Alsace. They had no intention of sustaining royal authority in France by force of arms ; their concern, on the contrary, would be rather to guard their own troops from the corruption of revolutionary doctrines. It was indeed obvious enough to Fronsac, as to all those not carried away by political passion, that any attempt at an invasion of France by German troops would merely result in the destruction of the royal family and probably most of the nobility as well. The rabid insistence of the French *émigrés* on armed intervention and on the formation of a league against their own country had therefore merely shocked the Germans and had made the French detested in Frankfort.

In this not very pleasant atmosphere, Fronsac's thoughts began to turn from Frankfort to Vienna. Before his return to France he was proposing to attend the Emperor's coronation as King of Hungary, and it would be an excellent opportunity to revisit Vienna on his way there and back.

CHAPTER V

BAPTISM OF FIRE

FRONSAC left Frankfort at the end of October 1790, and after journeying pleasantly through the richest and most fertile part of the Palatinate, reached Heidelberg, where a number of French refugee families were living. There he sent back his horses and took the post coach for Vienna, where he renewed his contacts with many old friends, including the Prince de Ligne and his son Charles, who like Fronsac was longing to see some active service.

There seemed at that time no particular prospect of their wishes being realised, but one night in November Fronsac was dining with the Prince de Ligne when a courier arrived bearing despatches from the Russian army which was then operating against the Turks. Ever since the days of Peter the Great, Russia had been struggling to expand her southern frontiers at the expense of the Ottomans, and the Empress Catherine was continuing this policy in a drive against Turkish strongpoints along the Black Sea coast. The fortress of Otchakov had been stormed in December 1788, and in the following year Catherine's favourite, Potemkin, had taken Akerman. But the fortress of Ismail, situated on the Danube delta some fifty miles from its mouth, still remained in Turkish hands.

The messenger who had just arrived from Russian headquarters brought despatches for the Prince de Ligne from his old comrade-in-arms, Potemkin, and was able to give the two young men the latest news of the operations. It appeared that the Russians had now decided to turn their attention to Ismail, the one important Turkish fortress remaining in that region, and the Russian army was at that very time preparing for an onslaught upon it. The two eager young soldiers

looked at each other in sudden excitement. " Let us go ! "
cried Fronsac. " It would be cowardly to hold back ! "
replied Charles de Ligne with equal enthusiasm. They
decided that there was not a moment to be lost ; they must
set off as soon as possible or everything would be over before
they got there. Charles de Ligne, who held the rank of colonel
in the Austrian army would first have to go to Presburg in
order to get special leave from the Emperor. But as soon as
he returned, they set off on their journey : a 1250-mile
steeplechase across almost desert country in the depths of
winter, nine days of non-stop travel in open post-chaises, with
little more baggage than what they carried on their backs.
Langeron, who was returning to the army, travelled with them.

Their route lay across part of Austria, Moravia, Silesia and
Galicia. Between Bielitz and Kenty they crossed the little
river which was the old Austro-Polish frontier, and at that
point there were obvious signs that they had left German
territory behind. The wooden houses with their pillared
porticoes, the strange clothes and shaven heads of the men
gave unmistakable evidence that they had entered eastern
Europe. At Tarnov they had to abandon one of their vehicles
which was holding them back and took turns in travelling
partly by the local post transport—which consisted of nothing
better than springless carts completely open to the weather.
But our three warriors could think of nothing but their
agonised fear of reaching the battlefield too late, and having
reached Lemberg, the capital of Galicia, they left their last
remaining vehicle to follow on as best it could and took
entirely to the postal carts. It was precisely at Lemberg that
the highroad from Vienna came to an end, and for the 200
miles on to Czernowitz the going was, as Fronsac admits,
" detestable." It was made even worse by the bitter cold and
the iron-hard frozen ground. By this time the three knights
errant had not been to bed for five nights. They were scarcely
half-way on their journey, and the worst part of it was still to
come. But not for a moment did their spirits flag—not even
when they were overturned into a ditch full of snow in the

middle of the night! After crossing the Dniester, they soon afterwards entered the province of Bukovina, recently taken from the Turks by the Emperor Joseph. Here nearly all the former inhabitants had removed themselves and the province had been repopulated by emigrants from different parts of Germany. Pressing on through beautiful wooded country and a little cultivated land, the trio entered Moldavia, where Fronsac's observant eye had time to note that the men in this region dressed like the Turks except for their headgear, which was a fur cap like the Poles, while the women were dressed like Greeks. The three travellers dined one evening with a local headman, who spoke passable Italian and from whom they gathered that the inhabitants regretted Turkish rule, Moldavia having been occupied by the Russians since the beginning of the war. At last, on the 20th November, after nine days and ten nights of rapid and strenuous travel, the three young soldiers reached Jassy, the Moldavian capital. But still oppressed with the need for haste, they stopped only long enough for the briefest rest and to give Langeron time to go on ahead with letters to Potemkin. Pressing on again after this short pause, they finally reached Bender, the Russian headquarters. Here they met Roger de Damas, who filled them with dismay by informing them that the campaign was over, and that he was on the point of leaving for France. However he cheered them a little afterwards by saying that there was still some idea of making an attempt on Ismail, and they decided to call on Prince Potemkin and present themselves to him without further delay.

Potemkin was installed in the pasha's house, but even so they were scarcely prepared for the strange scene which met their eyes. At one end of the large room, lit by numerous candles, some fifty officers of all ranks were standing about; but upon a large cloth-of-gold divan under an ornate canopy there reclined five elegantly attired women. A sixth, in a resplendent Greek costume, was sitting on cushions in the oriental manner, and the commander-in-chief sat beside her. Potemkin was clad in a large jacket similar to a dressing-gown;

it was his favourite, often his only, garment. It appeared that when he went to war, he had to be accompanied not only by a bevy of women but by well-served tables with an army of servants in attendance, and even by comedians, dancers and an orchestra. He received the three young men ceremoniously, but at first with a certain chilly reserve which seemed to denote suspicion.

In these curious surroundings the next three days were passed, while preparations for the attempt on Ismail were being completed. For by the end of November it had become clear that if the Russians were to obtain reasonably good peace terms they would need to have Ismail in their hands. Catherine therefore had imperiously ordered Potemkin to take it. The Prince de Ligne had sent a letter to his old comrade-in-arms, Potemkin, which stirred the Russian's interest both in Charles de Ligne and in his companions. He promised them that they should be sent to the front as early as practicable, and in fact a few days later they were attached to the corps of 5000 men commanded by Lieutenant-General Samoilov.

The fortress town of Ismail, situated on the left bank of one of the arms of the Danube, was built in a great semi-circle of which the Danube formed the diameter. The town had already been captured in the previous round of the struggle with Russia, but since then the Turks, appreciating the strategic importance of its position near the mouth of the Danube, had called in a French engineer to design proper fortifications on Western lines. Unfortunately for the Turks, the engineer, Delafitte, had been recalled to France before he had finished his work, and the Turkish engineer who succeeded him so little understood the principles of European fortification that on finding the great store of palisades left behind by Delafitte, he planted them in the middle of the rampart parapets, instead of inclining them on the outside edge at an angle which would have made the storming of the ramparts almost impossible. Fronsac indeed considered that this was one of the most important factors in the successful outcome of the attack on the town.

The Russian operations were chiefly marked in the beginning by indecision and vacillation, the fatal results of a divided command. The Danube flotilla, containing on board its numerous types of river vessels some 4000 men, was under the command of General Ribas, a forceful and enterprising Spaniard who had entered the Russian service. His two colleagues in command of the land forces, Gudovitch and Paul Potemkin—the latter a mediocre nephew of the commander-in-chief—were mainly distinguished by their inertia, which came near to wrecking the whole enterprise. Completely underestimating the toughness and tenacity of the enemy (a common Russian failing which was to prove costly on this, as on other occasions), the commanders of the land forces were under the persistent delusion that a hearty bombardment would be quite sufficient to frighten the Turks into surrendering the fortress and that no other serious effort would be required. Hence they arrived not only without any equipment for a long siege, but entirely ignorant of the strength and quality of the Turkish garrison, which according to Roger de Damas was in greater part composed of Janissaries and the pick of the Grand Vizier's army. Not only had they no information about the enemy, but they had very little about each other, the various commanders acting largely as independent units. General Ribas had soon come to the conclusion that the only way to take the place would be by storm, but he was unable to convert his colleagues to his point of view, even after the failure of a first artillery duel which had merely occasioned heavy losses to the Danube flotilla without making any impression on the defenders of the fortress. At a second conference, Ribas pressed his point of view again, but all the land commanders would agree to was that a feint attack should be made while the bombardment was intensified by larger numbers of ships and by the batteries set up on shore. If this did not succeed they were determined to abandon the undertaking, since Count Suvorov was only awaiting the arrival of Ribas to attack Brahilov, a well-fortified Turkish town near the Danube. This feeble plan was therefore carried out, with the sole result that one or two Turkish batteries were silenced. The red flag continued to fly defiantly over the town, and an immense number of small flags of all colours made their appearance, in undaunted challenge, on the ramparts.

But Ribas was not to be defeated either by the Turks or by the ineptitude of his colleagues. While the troops were falling back and a part of the fleet had already set sail, a messenger arrived at full speed from Prince Potemkin, whom Ribas had secretly informed of the state of affairs. Potemkin approved absolutely of Ribas' proposal to attack the town. He was not only to attack it, he was to take it ; failure was not even to be contemplated—which was all typically Potemkin. Furthermore, supreme command of the land forces was to be given to Count Suvorov. So now the guns were disembarked again and the battery sights repaired ; the land forces moved up and reoccupied their camp. Fronsac and Charles de Ligne were lodged during this time in a double chaloupe of the Danube flotilla, where they inhabited a tiny cabin-like shelter in which there was not room to stand up.

A few days later, Suvorov arrived, characteristically, at full gallop astride a Cossack horse, without either tent or baggage. Léon de Rochechouart relates the startling circumstances of Fronsac's first meeting with this remarkable man. On his way to pay his respects to the new commander-in-chief, Fronsac observed a crowd of soldiers assembled in the middle of the camp. Approaching closer, he found them standing in a ring round a naked man who was leaping and performing violent gymnastic exercises on the grass, unde- terred by the icy-cold fog of early morning. " Who is this lunatic ? " enquired Fronsac of one of the bystanders. " The Commander-in-Chief, Count Suvorov," was the reply. The strange apparition now observed Fronsac in his French hussar's uniform and signing him to approach, enquired his name. " Ah," he observed, on being told, " the grandson of Marshal Richelieu. Well, what do you say to my way of taking the air ? There is nothing more wholesome. I advise you, young man, to imitate me ; it is a sure way of avoiding rheumatism." Whereupon the general gave two or three more leaps and then returned to his tent, leaving the young man in question quite speechless. Suvorov had previously introduced himself to a startled Roger de Damas by strolling into the Frenchman's tent clad in nothing but a shirt. Fronsac gives an interesting account of " this strange man, who resembles more a Cossack or Tartar chieftain than the general of a European army." Suvorov's courage, said Fronsac, made him ignore all the recognised rules of war ; which only confirmed for the Russians their basic conviction of the uselessness of ordinary precautions or scientific method when fighting an enemy such as the Turks. Suvorov's great principle was that a swift knock-out blow would determine the result of a campaign right away, and in the long run would cost fewer men than a series of protracted and perhaps indecisive operations. The bayonet was therefore his favourite weapon, and an order to besiege a place was in his eyes merely another way of saying that it was to be taken by storm. Suvorov's mode of life was as unorthodox as his military opinions. He dined between six and eight in the morning, sitting on the ground in his tent ; the same meal would serve him as supper in the afternoon, and he would then sleep for a few hours. Damas, who had been invited to dine with the Russian general, relates how he duly presented himself at 6 p.m., only to be told by an adjutant that Suvorov had gone to bed. On waking, the general would often spend the rest of the night singing, and at daybreak would sally forth naked for his strenuous physical jerks. He possessed no horse of his own, but when he wished to make a reconnaissance would merely seize the first Cossack horse that came to hand, leap upon it and depart at full gallop, regardless of gunfire or of the danger of being taken by the enemy. He was genial in manner, invincibly cheerful, and had always been extraordinarily successful in his campaigns. This had invested him in the eyes of his soldiers with a kind of superstitious halo.

When speaking of the Russian soldier in general, Fronsac pays high tribute to the courage and patience with which

Russian troops would endure hardships which other nations would have found unbearable, and that when their only food was a little oatmeal, without bread, meat or vegetables. Yet in spite of this sparse diet, he found them just as physically robust as the Austrians, whose armies were then considered to be the best fed, and he considered this frugality of living to be one of the most important qualities of the Russian, which together with his bravery and obedience to his officers made him the best soldier in Europe. He further adds that no European soldier was more constantly gay than the Russian, who was capable of singing for five or six hours on end without interruption. He had, however, no such high opinion of the Russian officers, or of the generals' knowledge of warfare, and he considered that the greatest blot on the character of the Russian army as a whole was their total disregard of the welfare of their men. This, he thought, derived mainly from a fundamental indifference to the value of human life and partly also from the knowledge that conscription would soon make good any losses.

Suvorov now gave Ribas the longed-for order for a general attack. The fortress was to be surrounded, the troops closing in round it. This was promptly done and scaling ladders were constructed. All these preparations were watched with the greatest interest by the Turks who, with a strangely detached curiosity, crowded on to the ramparts in their colourful costumes to observe what was going on. Fronsac relates that upon the two gates of the town facing towards the Russian camp there were two kiosks in which the Pasha and his staff were accustomed to spend the greater part of each day smoking and watching the Russian activities. Nothing, it appeared, was suffered to interrupt this very important part of the daily programme, and they would remain placidly there throughout the heaviest bombardments, exposing themselves quite unnecessarily to the greatest risk.

The Turks having replied with a proud refusal to a final summons to surrender, the great assault began, after a further twenty-four-hour bombardment, to which the Turks replied with vigour and with telling effect, since the *Constantine*, the second brigantine of the flotilla, was hit and blew up with the loss of all on board. The attack was to be made by nine columns of infantry, the cavalry being kept in reserve. Roger de Damas was placed in command of two battalions of the extreme right-hand column, while Charles de Ligne commanded two battalions of Chasseurs in Brigadier Markov's column, whose task was to attack the stone bastion which was one of the most prominent parts of the fortifications. Since Fronsac did not wish to be separated from his friend, he accompanied that column as a volunteer. Ribas had wished for the attack to be at dawn rather than in the darkness, fearing possible confusion in a night attack ; but he was as usual overborne by his colleagues, though his fears turned out to be only too well grounded.

When the troops embarked in flat boats and chaloupes on the Danube, the night was an extremely dark one, with a thick fog. But they had not progressed very far down the river before the fog commenced to lift and revealed their movements to the Turks. The latter had been warned by a deserter of the coming assault and had been standing to arms all night. They now opened fire all along the perimeter of the fortifications and were supported by musketry fire along the entire length of the ramparts. The whole town, says Fronsac, looked like a volcano, and drama was added to the scene by a universal cry of " Allah ! " which rose from the defenders. Prince Charles de Ligne, who was standing at the end of his boat ready to jump ashore, was hit on the left knee by a musket ball with such violence that he would have been knocked down but for the support of Fronsac and a sergeant. In spite of his pain, he sprang ashore, together with Fronsac, through a hail of balls and grapeshot which cost the Russians heavy casualties. Nevertheless they formed into columns in good order and advanced to the attack, in face of a withering fire from the stone bastion. Fronsac had his cap traversed by a ball, luckily without its doing more than grazing his head. But by this time, Charles de Ligne was in such agony with his damaged knee that he could struggle on no farther. They were obliged to put him back on to the sole remaining boat which was still alongside the river bank, while he wept with vexation to see himself thus put out of the fight when it had scarcely begun. Fronsac, who took his place at the head of the column, now found himself in the awkward predicament of being alone in charge of troops whose language he could not speak. However, they were presently called upon to move up in support of the Black Sea Grenadiers who were in danger of being overwhelmed. Passing up to the front of the main column, they fought their way into the town, among narrow streets where it was impossible to keep formation and where the Turks, defending themselves inch by inch with stubborn determination, inflicted heavy losses on the invaders. Fronsac was hit a second time, but again his luck held and the ball did no more than tear his tunic.

By degrees, the Russians gradually penetrated everywhere into the defences and at last they encircled the main bastion where the Turkish commander made his final stand. With his sabre in one hand and a pistol in the other, he stood proudly at the head of his men, but strange to relate surrounded by musicians, who were actually playing their instruments in the very midst of the battle. An English naval officer who was present as a volunteer attempted to take the Turkish commander prisoner, but the Turk shot him dead. Whereupon, like the Gauls of old in the presence of the Roman senators, the Russian troops, who had paused uncertainly, now hurled themselves upon the garrison and regardless of the appeals of their officers, slaughtered the Turks to the last man. A strange feature of the affair was that these Turks, who numbered three or four thousand, seem to have made little attempt to defend themselves, but accepted their end with stoic fatalism.

Fronsac estimates that over 30,000 Turks perished altogether at Ismail, of whom at least 2000 were women and children. He himself saved the life of a small girl of eight, the sole survivor of a group of four women. The child was

very richly dressed and curious to relate wore round her neck
a gold chain and medal bearing an image of the French King.
She was obviously someone of high rank, since when she was
sighted by a group of Turks negotiating their surrender from
another bastion, they made a great clamour to have the child
returned to them. Fronsac handed her over on the definite
understanding from the Russian officer in charge of the
negotiations that she should be restored to him the following
day ; but he never set eyes on her again, and so the mystery
of her identity was never solved. As for the Turkish commander in this bastion, after his surrender he caused some
rugs to be spread out over the smoking ruins and then sat
smoking with as much philosophical calm as if he had been
in his own home. Nor were his officers any less impassive,
except at the actual moment of having to give up their arms ;
then the eyes of some among them filled with angry tears,
while others tried to break their weapons. In a house near
the main bastion a young boy of fourteen, the sole survivor
of his family, was also found sitting on a heap of cushions
placidly smoking, apparently oblivious of the frightful scenes
which had been enacted round him. He was sent to St.
Petersburg, where the Empress treated him well.

The booty captured at Ismail was immense, since the town
contained not only many wealthy inhabitants, but was filled
with wealthy refugees from other places. Priceless materials
and gaily coloured tents were to be seen scattered about the
streets, and numbers of beautiful horses, some of them the
Sultan's property, were running wild about the town, terrified
by the noise. In the midst of this nightmare scene, Fronsac
suddenly came upon Roger de Damas on one of the ramparts ;
they were both greatly relieved to find one another alive and
to know that Charles de Ligne and Langeron had also
survived.

Thus Fronsac had at last received the baptism of fire for
which he had been longing—even if the reality had dimmed
the glory. For a place taken by storm could never have been
a pleasant sight, and both Langeron and Damas in their

memoirs give a horrible picture of the sacked town, its streets
piled with corpses of all ages and both sexes, so that the very
mud in which the bodies lay was dyed red. Looking back
upon the Ismail operations afterwards, however, Fronsac
could not resist commenting upon some of its strange aspects
from a military point of view : the complete inaction of over
36,000 Turkish troops in face of the relatively small Russian
force of 23,000 ; the failure of the Turks to prevent the construction of the batteries to be used against them, or on their
side to make use of their numerous ships which could have
transported troops from the other side of the Danube. He
considered that in individual valour the Turk was the superior
of the European soldier, but was completely lacking in any
idea of the order and discipline without which valour is of
little use. But neither were the Russians without grave faults.
Their negligence and their contempt for the enemy made them
consider all the usual military precautions superfluous and
they were completely indifferent to the loss of life resulting
from their own carelessness. As an instance of this, Fronsac
particularly mentions their behaviour when taking up positions during the night for the construction of the batteries
which were to bombard the town. During this operation,
the Russians were talking and shouting loudly, and since the
soldiers had failed to bring up the constructional material,
the Russian officers had it brought up in creaking ox carts
which could be heard miles away. This not unnaturally
resulted in the firing of a broadside from the defenders on the
ramparts, causing some confusion and panic among the
Russians ; but fortunately the firing died down again almost
as quickly as it had begun. As a result of the Russians' careless indifference, however, their casualties at Ismail amounted
to more than half their officers and a third of their men. It
was not of course to be expected that they would display any
greater concern over the fate of their prisoners, who were
marched from Ismail to Bender ; the road was littered with
their corpses, those who fell out through weakness on the
march being promptly finished off by the Cossack escort.

As soon as Charles de Ligne's leg was well enough for him to travel, the little band of knights-errant decided to move on to Bender, on their way to Jassy. In the end, however, Damas and Fronsac had to leave their companion in a village through which they passed, while they went on ahead to arrange a lodging for him, since his leg was still giving him great pain. In Bender they were received, now most cordially, by Potemkin, who almost directly afterwards set off for Jassy with the intention of spending part of the winter there before returning to St. Petersburg. Damas, Fronsac and Langeron followed him there the same evening.

Jassy, the capital of Moldavia, was a pleasant town situated on two hills, very Turkish in its mode of life. The population, both men and women, spent most of their time sitting cross-legged on sofas, drinking coffee like the Turks. They also had the Turkish love of bathing, their baths being on much the same principle as those of the Turks. The boyars, says Fronsac, were by no means as ignorant and stupid as the Russians liked to make out ; but he found the women unattractive in their ugly, heavy costumes. This, however, did not prevent our three enterprising warriors from spending a week of much entertainment and gaiety in Jassy ; Roger de Damas, in particular, was never one to let the grass grow under his feet in this direction, and we may suspect that under his exuberant influence even the diffident Fronsac was prised out of his shell. After which light interlude, the trio took the road back to Vienna, Roger de Damas giving the other two a lift in his carriage for the journey, which this time was completed at considerably less breakneck speed.

They reached Vienna at the end of January 1791, to find the city *en fête* for the double marriage of two of the archdukes with the princesses of Naples, granddaughters of Maria Theresa. Damas, however, could not help noting with pain the changed language already being used in this year of 1791 by the French ambassador, the Marquis de Noailles. No more now was there any talk, in the time-honoured diplomatic phrase, of " the will of the King, my master " ; its place had been taken by a strange new jargon full of such expressions as " the nation," "decrees," "constitution," while Frenchmen in Vienna were actually being advised to wear tricolour cockades. All this must have been just as painful to Fronsac, and it was not long before he removed himself to St. Petersburg, where the Prince of Nassau, an admiral in the Russian service, presented him to the Empress Catherine. She received him with great favour, bestowing upon him the Order of St. George, together with a golden sword. She also made him a colonel, a higher rank than he held in the French army, and he was even admitted to the gatherings of her intimate circle at the Hermitage. This was an unusual honour for so young a man—but then Fronsac was a good-looking young man.

While he was thus basking in the sunshine of the imperial favour, however, news reached him from France that his father had died—which, said the gossips, was no loss. Though this event made him head of the family and brought him an inheritance of 500,000 francs, the money was encumbered with a crushing load of paternal debts, the settlement of which he considered to be his first duty. The Duc de Richelieu, as we must henceforth call him, was therefore obliged to hasten back to France.

CHAPTER VI

FROM PILLAR TO POST

In France meanwhile the political barometer continued its catastrophic plunge downward, and when in the spring of 1791 the King recalled Richelieu from a short visit to England in order that he might take his place in the depleted ranks of the royal household, the duke wrote to his wife with a sort of grim humour that to return to Paris under the prevailing conditions required more courage than to go into action at Ismail. But he was thus at his post in June, when the royal family made their ill-starred attempt at flight. Richelieu had been told nothing of their plan beforehand and only learned of it from one of the King's valets ; but the man was unable to tell him even which way they had gone. Deeply hurt at what he looked upon as a lack of confidence—as he himself had little confidence in his own capabilities he was for ever thinking that others felt the same about him—he went off to see his wife Rosalie at Courteilles. The next day, however, on hearing of the royal family's arrest and enforced return to Paris, he at once returned to his post.

There was little enough that a First Gentleman of the Bedchamber could do, at a Court which had now almost ceased to exist, but he could still be of service to the King through his connections with the outside world, and with Vienna in particular. Richelieu's father-in-law had died in May, and Rosalie wrote that her husband had shown himself as kind and thoughtful towards her than as during the time of her previous bereavement. When in August she went to take the waters at Chaufontaine, he escorted her half-way there, and then set out once more for Vienna on a special mission to the Austrian Cabinet. We do not know the exact nature of this mission, but there can be little doubt that it was connected with the secret contacts being maintained at this time between the Courts of Paris and Vienna.

But a keen soldier could not remain content with diplomatic activity when there was work for his sword, and the following year found Richelieu with the army of Condé, under whom he served in the campaign of 1792 which ended in the inglorious collapse of the Royalist forces. Austria having announced that she would be unable to provide further pay for the remnants of Condé's army after the following spring, the Empress Catherine sent an offer to Condé through Richelieu of 60,000 gold ducats for the *émigré* corps if they would be willing to settle as military colonists on the shores of the Sea of Azov, in the territories of Ekaterinoslav and the Tauride peninsula. The nobles among them, she declared, should have equal rights with the Russian nobility, while the Prince de Condé and his family would rank above all the Tsarina's own subjects. But those to whom exile from Paris was already an affliction scarcely to be borne were not likely to reconcile themselves to permanent settlement in a barbaric wilderness on the farthest frontiers of Europe, and notwithstanding the desperate circumstances of the *émigrés*, the offer was received with cold scorn. Probably too, their attitude was stiffened by the fact that Austria had now announced that she would resume payment of their army. Condé offered Richelieu the command of one of the corps, the Chevaliers de la Couronne, but by this time Richelieu had seen enough of the *émigrés* to decline the proposal and return to Vienna. Though Austria, owing to the difficulties of her political situation, did not wish to have Frenchmen serving in her army, it was announced that Russians personally recommended by the Empress Catherine would always be welcome, and it was therefore as Russian officers attached to the Austrian staff that Richelieu and Langeron took part in the campaigns of 1793–4 in the Low Countries and on the Rhine. Prince Charles de Ligne's thirst for military glory had already brought him to an untimely end ; he had been killed in the previous year fighting against Dumouriez. The Empress Catherine charged Richelieu and Langeron with the task of transmitting daily reports on the course of operations, and these they sent to her through her representative in Brussels.

But although Richelieu, on leaving France again, had been careful to get official permission to do so, not only from the King but from the National Assembly, there could now be no denying that he was in arms against the French Republic, even though, like other French nobles, he might consider that his true allegiance lay to the cause of the fallen Bourbon monarchy. He had therefore become an *émigré*, and his property was forfeit to the State. In spite of the efforts made by the duchess to save the family domains, the Convention declared the Richelieu estate, including the château, to be national property. Much of it was sold, and Rosalie, who had thus unfortunately drawn attention to her own existence, was thrown into prison, from which she was only released by the fall of the Convention. Much of her mother's property at Courteilles was also sequestered, though the château itself survived and escaped pillage even during the Terror. For the duchess, her mother and grandmother were much loved in the neighbourhood for their numerous charitable activities, and one of the local revolutionaries, a man by name of Simon, proved to be a friend in need. When rioters burst into the château, he placed himself at their head, and while making a show of speaking loudly and roughly to " the woman Richelieu," he added at the same time under his breath : " Mme la duchesse, give them something to drink and I will look after the rest." It is pleasant to know that Simon had the good fortune to survive the Revolution, and was able to end his days in comfortable retirement living on the means provided for him by grateful aristocrats whom he had protected.

Meanwhile the campaign in the Low Countries was brought to an inglorious conclusion, dissension and incompetence among the German allies proving no match for the fiery impetus of the French Republican armies. When the

Austrian army was driven back behind the Rhine, Richelieu returned to Vienna for the winter of 1794-5, and then set out again for Russia in the spring with Langeron. Their friend, Count Andrew Razumovski, the Russian ambassador in Vienna, wrote to Prince Zubov, the Empress Catherine's latest favourite, expressing the hope that the services rendered by the two Frenchmen might entitle them to some help and consideration in view of the difficult circumstances in which they now found themselves placed.

By that time there was a considerable colony of French *émigrés* living in St. Petersburg. They had been there since the first years of the Revolution, just as a century and a quarter later the picture was to be reversed when the Russian aristocracy came to Paris as refugees from another revolution. The Prince de Ligne, speaking of the portrait painter, Mme Vigée-Lebrun, who arrived in St. Petersburg in 1795, said that she would " soon think herself in Paris, there are so many French in the gatherings." The *émigré* colony brought with them their mode of life : on the one hand, the rather childish amusements of the Court of Marie-Antoinette, charades, riddles, rhymes and various games ; but, on the other, the life of the *salon*, which they introduced into Russian society, bringing it into closer touch with the literature and thought of the West. Alongside the aristocratic emigration there was also an ecclesiastical one, which brought a number of clerical teachers both to St. Petersburg and to Moscow, chief among them the Abbé Nicolle, who came to Russia in the spring of 1793 with the Comte de Choiseul's younger son, whose tutor he was. Many of the Abbé's former colleagues of the Collège Sainte Barbe joined him in St. Petersburg, to the great benefit of the children of the Russian nobility. The Abbé Nicolle set an entirely new precedent by the foundation of an Institute for these children, since hitherto it had been quite unknown for children of the upper classes to go outside their own homes for their education. By 1802, his Institute had become famous throughout Russia.

Old Marshal Rumiantsov had offered Richelieu the

appointment of lieutenant-colonel in the Cuirassiers of St. George, and to Langeron a position of the same rank in the Little Russian Grenadiers. But when they presented themselves at the Court of St. Petersburg in the spring of 1795, they found conditions sadly changed. The Bourbon monarchy had ceased to exist, and French nobles were at a discount—particularly as many of the refugees whom the Empress had allowed to settle in St. Petersburg had repaid her by permitting their *salons* to become centres of malicious gossip directed against her. Richelieu thus found himself in as embarrassing a situation as he and Caraman had been in Frankfort ; as on that occasion, he had to suffer for the behaviour of his countrymen. No longer was he invited to the gatherings at the Hermitage ; though when the Empress received Langeron and himself one day at Tsarkoëselo, she had greeted them with all her usual graciousness. It appeared that the animosity shown to them sprang rather from the members of her Court, for Prince Zubov, to whom Razumovski had written on their behalf, was bitterly hostile, as were all those round him, and it was made clear to the two Frenchmen that the place of two newly appointed colonels was with their regiments. They lost no time, therefore, in departing to take up their duties, their regiments being stationed at Dubno, in a province of Poland recently occupied by Russia after the Second Partition. From there, Langeron wrote bitterly to Prince Andrew Razumovski : " I cannot tell you the humiliations, the rudenesses, the rebuffs, of which we were the objects." But for the necessity of settling his debts he would not, he said, have remained in St. Petersburg at all, " and nothing can explain to me how Richelieu stood it ! " Actually, Richelieu himself had already written to Razumovski from St. Petersburg, saying much the same about the reception they had had ; poverty and misfortune could be borne, he said, but humiliation never. Yet, as Langeron continued in his letter to Razumovski, the Russians when speaking of the French in their midst, would say : " Ah, but these two are different ; we have nothing against them." Judge then, remarked

Langeron caustically, what the position of the others must be ! However, he and Richelieu, it appeared, were leading a peaceful enough life in Poland ; the only blemish on it was the thought of the two months that would have to be spent in St. Petersburg. Richelieu, said Langeron, had had the great good fortune to find a teacher of Russian in the regiment, and with the aid of his prodigious memory capable of learning 500 new words in a day would no doubt be speaking fluent Russian in about three months, especially as none of those around him could speak French. Louis XVIII had written to inform Richelieu that he would not recall him for the present—which meant to say that he had at the same time no intention of losing track of the duke.

Soon after this time Richelieu's regiment was transferred to Novgorod and it was while they were there that an event occurred which was to be of the greatest significance in his life. The Grand Duke Alexander came to review the troops, and had his first meeting with the regiment's colonel. The Russian historian Bogdanovich has said of Alexander that his character was composed of a number of sharply contrasting and changeable elements, but that above all these he possessed a remarkable ability to charm the hearts of all with whom he came into contact. His charm probably owed a good deal to his handsome physical presence : he was tall and well built, with large blue eyes and fair, curly hair. But woven into his complex nature there was undoubtedly, too, a strong thread of idealism. This had been encouraged by his upbringing, since his education had been carefully based by his grandmother, as befitted a sovereign of the Age of Enlightenment, on the same humanitarian precepts of French philosophy as had been imbibed by the Emperor Joseph II of Austria. A community of thought and interest thus quickly forged a strong link between Richelieu and Alexander, and their meeting marked the beginning of the lifelong friendship which was to play such an important part in the duke's future career.

But the death of the Empress Catherine in the following

year was a real misfortune for Richelieu, and to add to his ill-luck Marshal Rumiantsov soon followed his sovereign to the grave. " He did everything for me," wrote Richelieu to Razumovski, " and would always have supported me." Although by 1797 Richelieu had become a major-general through seniority, and was in command of the Emperor's Cuirassiers, the more than half-mad Tsar Paul detested the regiment, which he thought to have been filled with his mother's spies, and during the three years following her death he vented his spite on the regiment's unfortunate commanding-officer. The Tsar, whose ideal of military perfection was the Prussian army, had a mania for continual parades, and above all for impeccable correctness in the uncomfortable Prussian-type uniform which he had imposed on his soldiers. It must be confessed that such details were never Richelieu's strong point. Though he took great care of his hands, which were fine and very well shaped, he was always apt to be careless about matters of dress. In the years to come he was to shock the more elegant of his compatriots in Paris by appearing on social occasions in boots and by his habit of smoking a pipe. He was thus only too vulnerable a target for the Tsar's end-less reprimands which raged like thunderstorms about him, often in front of his men. The final explosion came when on his own initiative he had taken his regiment to the help of a burning village. Paul stormed at him in front of the whole Court, accusing him of indiscipline, and then deprived him of his command. Richelieu, feeling that his position had become impossible, resigned his commission and left Russia for Poland.

During the ensuing months, the duke passed what must have been one of the darkest periods of his life. With financial resources which amounted to hardly more than thirty sous a day, he lived in Poland without proper employment and with very little prospect of any. Return to France was not yet possible—if indeed it ever would be—and now it seemed that Russia, where he had begun to make himself a career, was also henceforth to be closed to him. But like the dawn which follows the darkest night, a dramatic change came about in Richelieu's fortunes at the beginning of 1801. In March of that year, the Tsar Paul was assassinated by a group of nobles who felt called upon to rid Russia of the nightmare rule of a capricious madman, and the crown was transferred to the head of the Grand Duke Alexander. The new Tsar, a good friend to Richelieu even if a baffling human enigma to the rest of Europe, at once recalled the duke to St. Petersburg and promoted him to the rank of lieutenant-general.

Richelieu now began to consider the possibility of revisiting France in an attempt to get his name removed from the proscription list of *émigrés*. If he could succeed in doing this, he might be able to recover some at least of his confiscated property, and so be able to provide more adequately for his wife and sisters. He therefore made formal application through Kalitchev, the Russian chargé in Paris, and in 1801 Rosalie was able to write to him that Maret and Fouché had shown her a document, actually bearing the signature of the First Consul, authorising the removal of his name from the proscription list. He was thus free to return to Paris.

On the 2nd January 1802, Richelieu arrived in Paris, where he was welcomed joyfully by his wife and sisters. By a hideous irony of fate, both his sisters had by this time also become deformed, in a manner very similar to that of the unfortunate Rosalie. Needless to say, however, this had not prevented the arrangement of marriages for them, the elder one, Armandine, having been married in 1799 to the Marquis de Montcalm, and the younger, Simplicie, to the Comte de Jumilhac. Armandine's marriage did not turn out a success, and after giving birth to several children who all died after a few months of life, by 1805 she and her husband had parted. But Simplicie became the mother of two sons, the elder of whom, Odet de Jumilhac, was eventually to be the inheritor of his uncle's title.

Now that he had actually returned to Paris, on the assurance that his name would be removed from the list, Richelieu yet found that, for some mysterious reason, the authorisation

was being held up ; that, to his great disgust, he must go and
inscribe his name, as in an act of submission, at the Hôtel de
Ville, and that he was not allowed to wear either his uniform
or his foreign orders. Five months passed by without any
sign of the promised document, and Richelieu would not
make any overture himself. Only when he was within a
fortnight of leaving the country again could Rosalie persuade
him to let her approach Josephine at Malmaison. Madame
Bonaparte, as she then was, expressed surprise at the delay,
and promised that she would get the document sent by the
next day at the latest. She even rang the bell and enquired
if the First Consul were free, but was told he was in Council.
She again promised her help, however, and the Duchesse de
Richelieu departed feeling satisfied with her interview ;
though her husband took a less sanguine view when he heard
her account. His fears were well founded ; again nothing
further happened. Finally, the real purpose behind all these
strange manœuvres was unmasked : they desired him to
accept the new régime and to take service under it. Such was
the price asked for the removal of his name from the list of
émigrés. Richelieu was not prepared to pay that price, although
it meant leaving his womenfolk in difficult financial circumstances. In May 1802, he left France once more to return to
Russia, taking with him his wife's nephew, Ernest d'Aumont,
and his cousin, Charles de Rastignac. On the way, he wrote
to Rosalie from Vienna that he would never forget the
sensitive delicacy she had shown in her understanding of his
attitude, and that any sacrifices he should be in a position to
make in the future he would gladly make for her. On reaching St. Petersburg, the Tsar welcomed him back most cordially, and not only gave him the sum of 10,000 francs for his
immediate needs but also presented him with a small estate in
Courland which brought in an income of 12,000 francs, an
amount which was soon to double itself. Richelieu at once
wrote to his wife and mother-in-law, begging them to accept
this revenue. It was only just, he said, that as he by his
departure had been the cause of their financial ruin, he should

do what he could to help them ; especially as he himself could now manage quite well without the money.

It was soon after this that the Emperor Alexander again exerted his powerful influence on behalf of his friend, in a personal appeal to Napoleon for Richelieu's name to be removed from the list of *émigrés*. Since at that particular period Napoleon was anxious to cultivate good relations with the Tsar, the appeal did not on this occasion fall upon stony ground, and in a letter of the 11th February 1803 to Talleyrand, Richelieu was able to acknowledge receipt of the pleasing news. In a letter he wrote at the same time to the First Consul, he explained that the great kindnesses he had received from the Tsar placed him under an obligation to continue in the Russian service, but that in doing so he hoped to be also of some service to his own country and his compatriots. The advantage of having a liaison officer between himself and the Tsar was not lost upon Napoleon, and Richelieu was authorised to remain provisionally in Russia, provided he made a declaration that he would remain French and would return to France if ordered to do so. With regard to the settlement of his personal affairs, Richelieu had arranged for Rosalie to act for him. He was actually far more concerned with the settlement of his father's debts than about his own personal assets : " If there is nothing left for me," he told her, " at least I can hold up my head, and what I have I shall owe only to myself."

But the Emperor Alexander had not ceased to extend a helping hand to his friend. He was now about to open the door to an entirely new phase of Richelieu's career when in February 1803 he offered him the post of Governor of the newly founded Black Sea port of Odessa.

PART TWO

GOVERNOR-GENERAL

CHAPTER I

NEW-RUSSIA

By the opening years of the reign of Catherine the Great, the Russians in their drive south against the Turks had succeeded in reaching the Sea of Azov ; but the Black Sea coastline still remained in Ottoman hands. This part of Europe had a history stretching back into the days of classical legend, but the fanatical Moslems who had since swept over it had left it nothing but a depopulated desert, from which the Greeks, Armenians and Tartars who had colonised it had fled. The Crimea, inhabited in ancient times by the Scythians and then by the Greeks, had been overrun in 1237 by the Tartars, and by the end of the fifteenth century they had set up there a Tartar state under Turkish protection. Since then, the region had prospered, owing to its well-placed position on the Black Sea, its climate and its geographical features. For while the flat portion of the Crimean peninsula was a continuation of the steppes to the north, providing pasturage for large herds of animals but with the same rigorous climate as the Russian plains, beyond the mountain barrier which screened the southern half lay a region more typical of the Mediterranean : lovely and fertile valleys, luxuriating with flowers, fruit and vines.

Yet even though they had settled in this well-favoured land, the Tartars could not forego the habits of centuries, and their continual raids into Russian territory were a source of terror and misery to their neighbours. The raids had reached a climax of intensity in the first few years of Catherine's reign, at a time when she was preoccupied with Poland where many of her best troops were tied down. But in May 1783, Potemkin led an army across the Perekop isthmus, meeting with practically no resistance, and in July of the same year the Crimea was officially announced to be part of the Russian dominions. War having broken out again between Russia and Turkey in 1787, the storming by the Russians of the three great fortresses of Ozchakov, Akerman and Ismail between the years 1788 and 1790 gave Russia control of the mouths of all the great rivers—the Dnieper, Bug, Dniester and Danube—which debouched into the Black Sea. But the thread of Russian success was now interrupted by European complications, notably the French Revolution, and by the sudden death of Potemkin. Catherine decided to make peace with Turkey, and a treaty was signed at Jassy in January 1792. Under its terms, the Russian frontier was advanced to the Dniester, the fortress of Ozchakov (at the mouths of the rivers Bug and Dnieper) remained in Russian hands and the annexation of the Crimea by Russia was recognised.

Thus the territories which came to be known as New-Russia, extending from the Dniester to the Caucasus, were incorporated in the Moscovite Empire. The Comte de Ségur, who accompanied the Empress Catherine on her tour in 1787, gives an interesting description of their journey in that year through southern Russia on their way to the Crimea. They went down the Dnieper and " entered again what is called the Steppes, vast and lonely prairies absolutely devoid of trees and crossed at long intervals by a few bare hillocks watered at their base by shallow brooks. One may often travel eighteen or twenty miles without meeting a man, house or bush. Immense flocks of sheep and numerous troops of horses were the only objects to be seen in those dreary solitudes. The entire extent of the country from the Bug to the Sea of Azov . . . is nothing but an immense sea of verdure." It now remained to populate and bring to life these vast sandy deserts sprinkled with thin grass. In spite of its unprepossessing appearance, the soil was actually very fertile, and in the days of Greek colonisation full advantage had been taken of this. But the primitive nomads who had since swept over the region had known nothing of agriculture; nor was any settled rural life possible without security. To obtain this condition it was necessary to tame not only the Tartars but the turbulent Zaporozhski Cossacks, and also to keep at bay the Circassians, since these warlike people were in the habit of making constant irruptions across the Kuban river, the Russian frontier at the foot of the Caucasus. Catherine solved these two problems at one stroke by transplanting the Zaporozhski Cossacks after the destruction of their stronghold on the islands of the lower Dnieper, to the Kuban, where they were formed into a force of Black Sea Cossacks for the specific purpose of holding the Circassians in check. A measure of security was given to the Dnieper region by the construction of the fortress of Kherson and of the town of Ekaterinoslav (" Glory of Catherine "). The fortress of Kherson had almost been completed when Ségur visited the town in 1787 and he speaks of " a town already doing trade, with 2000 houses, shops full of merchandise from Greece, Constantinople and France, and about 200 trading vessels moored or coming into port." In the Crimea, the Tartar inhabitants were encouraged to turn their attention to such peaceful pursuits as fruit-growing and viticulture in their luxuriant valleys, or to the small industries of their ancient capital, Batchi-Serai. Though the ancient Greek fortress at Balaclava had been allowed to fall into ruin, the great new fortress of Sevastopol provided not only a military strongpoint but a naval base as well.

But Catherine realised that if the rest of her new dominions were not to remain mere tracts of sandy desert, new settlers must be found and induced to come in. She therefore sent agents abroad to recruit agricultural workers and artisans, turning her attention particularly to the Rhineland. Suitable types of immigrants were provided with facilities for travelling to Russia with their families in their great four-horse German wagons. A colonial committee was set up with headquarters at Ekaterinoslav, the chief centre of the first German settlements, and on the arrival of new colonists in

Russia the committee allocated to each family a stone-built house, a cow, a pair of oxen and a plough. An allowance was also provided on a graduated scale for each member of the family for the first year, until the head of the family was sufficiently well established to be able to maintain the household himself by his agriculture or his industry. Horses for the colonists were supplied by the Nogai Tartars, the last of the wandering Mongol tribes who still roamed north of the Crimea ; the money they received from the sale of horses would, it was hoped, be an incentive to them to settle down into a sedentary life. At the end of ten years, the land, the house and the garden of each family of colonists became their property. For the first twenty-five years after their arrival in Russia, the colonists were not called upon for any form of military service ; indeed the Mnemonists, a wealthy Anabaptist sect from East Prussia who brought all their riches with them and whose religious beliefs prohibited them from making war, received by imperial decree a permanent exemption from military service.

Many immigrants came from Wurtemburg, Swabia and Baden, so that along the shores of the Black Sea villages sprang up bearing such familiar names as Speyer, Landau, Worms and Strasbourg. Further along the coast towards the Crimea, in the Crimea itself and along the Sea of Azov, Greek colonists who had been encouraged to settle by Catherine busied themselves with the commerce they understood so well. There were also groups of Serbians and Bulgarians who had fled from Turkish oppression, Russians of strange religious sects, Armenians and Jews. Each colony was allowed the free exercise of its own religion, and it was also permitted to retain the municipal organisation to which it had been accustomed. Periodically the colonies were inspected by the Governor-General of New-Russia.

Since very early times, the Tartar hamlet of Hadji-Bey on the Black Sea coast had served as the port of embarkation for all the grain and merchandise with which Constantinople had been supplied across the Black Sea. The little town, surrounded with high crenellated walls, had been captured by the Russians in 1790, and the Empress Catherine had at once realised its potential value as a port, both commercial and military, for all south Russia. She decided to expand it for that purpose into a large town, and by a ukase of May 1792 she gave it the Greek name of Odyssos, which was soon Russianised into Odessa. Greeks, Italians, Bulgarians were encouraged to come and settle in the town. The erection of buildings began ; large sums were spent on a citadel, barracks and other necessary constructions. Streets were laid out, though without any settled plan. Nor was work on the port carried through to its conclusion, for in truth the attention of the Empress was presently diverted to other affairs, and the development of Odessa began to languish. The result was that the town gradually became a refuge for undesirable elements from all over the country. When Catherine died, Paul I, in complete ignorance as to the real condition of Odessa, thought to place it on the same footing as Riga and Revel by giving it a proper administrative machinery ; but what actually happened was that public appointments were farmed out among the gang of rogues who were running the town. For the specific purpose of enabling a pier and proper harbour facilities for large ships to be provided, the Tsar granted to Odessa exemption for a period of twenty-five years from all taxation and from the necessity of lodging troops, as well as providing a loan of 25,000 roubles free of interest. There was, however, no proper control over the town's finances. A committee of seven persons, including the mayor, was indeed formed to supervise the harbour construction, but they found themselves in a continual state of war with the municipality, whose members appear to have used the funds available for their own purposes.

By the time of Tsar Alexander's accession, therefore, not only had Odessa made no progress forward, but even such public buildings as had already been constructed—the quarantine station, the marine hospital, the citadel, the little pier—were falling into ruins, and the population, a mosaic of

Russians, Poles, Greeks, Armenians, Jews, Turks and Tartars, numbered little more than 4500. Charles Sicard, a Marseilles business man who came to Odessa and was to remain there for twenty-two years, gives a grim picture of the town as it was just before Richelieu's arrival. The houses were no more than huts covered with earth or straw; two thatched huts served as churches. While the inhabitants possessed a sufficiency of the most primary necessities, they completely lacked fruit or vegetables, since the countryside for miles around was uncultivated desert. There was, needless to say, no water supply in the town and hardly even any wells. Nor was there any wood for heating or building except what could be brought down the Dnieper via Kherson; few stone quarries were known. The revenue of the town was practically nil, in spite of the concession allowed on customs, for there was in truth practically no produce on which to levy any customs dues.

Such then was the depressing scene which confronted the newly made Governor of Odessa when he arrived to take up his duties at the beginning of 1803.

CHAPTER II

ODESSA

THE sight of Odessa and its surroundings might well have dismayed a man of lesser calibre than Richelieu, but the duke, far from being daunted by the magnitude of the task before him, accepted it as a challenge which called forth all his resources of energy and powers of organisation. For Odessa was too valuable in its potentialities to be allowed to fall into ruin. Its position on the Black Sea coast between the Dnieper and the Dniester made it the natural outlet for produce from the vast expanse of Russia's territory : the wheat, barley, flax, hemp, wood, butter, leather and sheepskin produced abundantly on the plains of Russia and Russian Poland. Up to the time of Richelieu's arrival in Odessa, trade between northern Europe and the East had had to travel via Dantzig and the Baltic—a long and costly route. The development of Odessa as a port would divert this huge current of trade to the Black Sea.

Richelieu's first task was to cleanse the municipality of the rascally gang which had for so long been lining their own pockets at the expense of the town. In their place was set up an administrative committee consisting of the mayor, two local business men, the commanding officer of the fortress, an engineer-officer, the quarantine inspector and the chief customs officer, with Richelieu himself acting as President. In consultation with the local notables, a careful assessment was then made of the resources and needs of Odessa, proper account being kept of the town's finances. The committee decided upon and saw carried out the public and municipal construction which was considered necessary and which had now become possible with the aid received from the government,

from whom Richelieu obtained a loan of 200,000 roubles for
the most primary necessities. The most urgent of these were
the port facilities : the quarantine station and the two piers,
one for ships coming from the Dnieper, the Black Sea or the
Sea of Azov with produce ; the other for foreign ships which,
having touched at Constantinople, had become subject to
quarantine. Work was begun on the port without delay, and
soon large quays and docks were under construction. Warehouses were also built for the storing of merchandise, and
since Richelieu saw that commerce would be the lifeblood of
the new town, he designed to sweep away many of the tiresome and arbitrary restrictions previously set up. Here, however, he was to find himself continually obstructed by the
bureaucratic Russian administration ; his correspondence re-
veals his irritation at the ill will and ignorant obstinacy with
which he frequently had to contend. In place of the old
system, he proposed that on all the corn exported a small tax
should be levied which was to be employed on such urgent
needs as the construction of roads, barracks, churches, etc.
This proposal was carried and the tax, gathered now by honest
collectors, soon brought in the sum of 12,000 roubles, which
enabled a start to be made on the work of building and re-
organisation. Richelieu caused the barracks to be moved from
their existing position on the sea front to the outskirts of the
town, where they would form a system of outer defences to
protect the town from surprise attack from the land side. He
had the quarantine station established in the old citadel, where
it could be isolated from the rest of the town, and a large
hospital was constructed. The spiritual needs of the population were provided for by the building of Roman Catholic and
Orthodox cathedrals, a synagogue and a Jesuit church, the
Emperor confiding to the Abbé Nicolle the care of all the
Catholic churches in south Russia. Since the Abbé made
Odessa his headquarters, his relations with the Governor soon
became cemented into the close friendship which was to
endure for the rest of Richelieu's life.

    To stimulate the erection of houses, sites were given free

by the town committee to those who wished to build, on condition that they did so within the space of two years, and that
during that time they planted at least 300 trees. This ensured
the creation out of uncultivated land of a pleasant green belt
round the town. Streets were laid out, of a width of fifty feet,
paved, lighted and also planted with trees. Richelieu was
particularly concerned with the growing of abundant greenery;
one tree more upon the desolate landscape, says Sicard, was to
the duke like one more soul in his dominions. The very first
tree to make its appearance was a poplar, planted by the
Chevalier de Rosset near the new quarantine station. Then
followed the laying-out of public gardens and a botanical
garden. Richelieu found both pleasure and relaxation from
more serious duties in the care of the newly planted vegetation,
often pruning and watering it with his own hands. He imported acacia seeds from Vienna at his own expense, distribu-
ting them to anyone anxious to plant them, and many did so to
please him. Sicard relates that a certain inhabitant of Odessa
had in front of his house two of these trees which were seen on
one occasion to be drooping from lack of water. The duke
paid him a visit and said to him : " I beg of you to give these
trees a little water. If you are not able to do so, permit me to
do it myself." In August 1804, Richelieu wrote to Rosalie
asking her to send him some seeds from the flowers and shrubs
which her grandmother, who had died at Courteilles in April
of that year, had tended there with such loving care, so that
he might sow them in memory of her in the garden he was
making at Odessa.

The whole administration of the town felt the impulsion of
the Governor's energy. In his spare time, Richelieu would
scour the town and the port, inspecting the work in progress
and spurring it on with his personal attention. He went about
always like a private person, on foot, on horseback or in a
droski, never in a closed carriage, even in the most severe
weather. He would visit the foreigners in quarantine, talking
to them and encouraging them to come and live in Odessa.
Charles Sicard tells how when he was in quarantine on his

arrival in the town, a high-ranking officer whom he later discovered to be the Governor approached him, enquired court-
eously about his health and the aim of his journey, and after
asking various questions about Marseilles and its inclination
to trade with the Black Sea, offered his services to Sicard whom
he invited to come and see him as soon as the quarantine period
should be over. Merchants of every nation were in fact personally received by Richelieu, who was able to talk to them
about their affairs with ease and knowledge, since as we have
seen he was widely travelled and spoke several European
languages with fluency. In this connection, he once related to
the Marquis de Castelnau, who was a member of his staff at
Odessa, how, when he was in Germany and was walking along
the ramparts of a town, he met an officer on patrol whom he
naturally addressed in German. But this produced no response
whatever, so the duke repeated his remarks in Italian, then in
English, and finally even in Russian. The sole result of his
efforts was to bring forth a plaintive enquiry, delivered with
the most villainous Gascon accent, as to whether he did not
know a word of French !

Not only did Richelieu receive merchants at his headquarters, but he also visited their shops in the town in order to
keep himself informed of their needs, and he made a particular
point of seeking out those who did not come to him. He
would often be seen to stop and talk in the streets with
peasants, discussing their affairs with them and advising them.
He was equally solicitous in visiting the captains of ships
which put in at Odessa, going round the port from one vessel
to another in a long boat. Sicard relates that on one occasion
Richelieu found in a French ship a little orphan cadet of only
eight or ten years of age whom he adopted, put to school and
set on the way to becoming in due course an officer.

The affability and understanding interest displayed by the
Governor of Odessa in his reception of new arrivals set the
tone of the whole administration down to the most minor
officials. It is clear, too, that Richelieu himself had travelled
a long way from the rather stiff and diffident young man

ODESSA IN THE NINETEENTH CENTURY

described by Langeron. His knowledge of practical affairs was a particularly valuable asset to a town situated so far from the headquarters of the imperial government. An even greater asset was Richelieu's personal friendship with the Tsar, which was to enable him on more than one occasion to cut his way through bureaucratic red tape by a direct appeal to the Sovereign.

In his work of establishing Odessa on a solid foundation, Richelieu did not omit to provide for future generations of its citizens. He lost no time in bringing into existence primary schools for boys and a school specially reserved for children of the Orthodox faith. Within a few years of his arrival in Odessa, he followed this up with the foundation of a secondary school or Gymnase for the sons of merchants, and an Institute for young people of noble birth. The latter foundation was from the beginning a success under the experienced direction of the Abbé Nicolle. The Gymnase was much less so, since merchants were unable to see the point of leaving their children at school for longer than was necessary to acquire the rudiments of education. A few years after its inception, therefore, Richelieu contemplated amalgamating it with the Institute as a Lycée. But this plan was only to come to fulfilment after he had left Russia.

The result of all this activity on the part of the Governor of Odessa was not long in becoming apparent. By 1808, the population of the town had risen to nearly 8000, and during that year 643 foreign ships used the port. By this time Odessa's exports and imports were going as far as Moscow, while Russian Poland, for which Odessa was the outlet port, had quadrupled her output of produce during the previous few years. When colonies of Bulgarians, Slavs and Germans established themselves in the environs of the town, Richelieu had a special quarter built to house those who were artisans, while the agricultural workers were distributed, with the aid of government subsidies, over the adjoining countryside. There Richelieu would inspect them from time to time, to see how they were getting on.

There were, of course, some of the usual grumblers who complained about what they called the " useless expenditure" of public revenue on the new developments. The duke, however, made a special point of visiting these potential trouble-makers and of having long talks with them, to show that he bore no ill feeling.

CHAPTER III

THE FIELD WIDENS

WHEN Richelieu had been twelve months in Odessa, he made the long journey north to St. Petersburg in order to discuss the town's affairs with the Tsar and give a first-hand account of its needs. So great was the hold that he had already acquired upon the affections of the people for whom he laboured that upon his return a great crowd from the town and the neighbouring villages came out fifty miles to welcome him back. The Tsar was equally appreciative of what Richelieu had already achieved in Odessa, since his own nobles showed little inclination to undertake any form of government service. Such matters, they observed complacently, were the exclusive concern of their sovereign—who, in a ukase of 1802, complained publicly and bitterly of their attitude. Alexander was thus frequently obliged to make use of foreigners, not only in the conduct of foreign affairs—in which his ministers included the Corsican, Pozzo di Borgo and the Greek, Capodistrias—but also in domestic administration. In Richelieu he found one who in addition to being both energetic and competent, shared many of his own enlightened principles. In 1805, therefore, he made the duke Governor-General of the whole territory of New-Russia.

Richelieu's new appointment placed him in control of an area almost as large as France, extending from the Dniester to the Kuban rivers, the latter marking the Russian frontier at the foot of the Caucasus. His work now included the direction and inspection of village colonies in the three areas of government which made up the province of New-Russia : Kherson, Ekaterinoslav and the Crimea. Over these areas were distributed some 36,000 people of various races, although drawn from the interior of Russia : Bulgarians, Germans, Greeks, Jews, and the curious Russian sect of the Dukobors. All these alien elements needed blending into an integral part of the Russian population, and Richelieu busied himself, as at Odessa, with touring the villages, talking to the people and informing himself of their needs.

As in the case of Odessa, the new territories were still largely a wilderness where everything needed to be done, but Richelieu threw himself into the task with his customary energy and enthusiasm. The most necessary preliminary to real development of the territory was the settlement of the nomadic elements which still lingered, chief among them the Nogai Tartars, the last wandering horde on the boundaries of Europe and Asia. Richelieu handed over the administration of these people to the Comte de Maisons, another French exile with as much energy and drive as himself. Maisons set to work on his task in a manner worthy of Richelieu, and in a few years nearly 100 villages had sprung up around the mosques he had built as an incentive to permanent settlement. Villages were surrounded by fields of corn and vegetables, while fishing and sheep rearing for wool soon brought the Tartars a regular income which was a powerful inducement to a settled life. In the area of the Kuban river, the Cossack settlements transplanted by Catherine from the Dnieper were by this time languishing. Since the typical Cossack lived only for fighting and plunder, scorning all domestic ties, their numbers were slowly but steadily dwindling until they were no longer in sufficient strength to fulfil their purpose of holding the Kuban frontier against the Circassians. Moreover, since they knew and cared nothing about agriculture, their land was unculti-vated and they lived in progressively increasing misery and want. Richelieu now transplanted into their midst a further 25,000 colonists from the Dnieper area, people originally Cossacks too, but who had acquired some measure of civilisa-tion and who migrated with their families. Revived by the infusion of this new blood, the colony was then given a proper military organisation and a training in cavalry tactics. Ten regiments of cavalry, ten of infantry, and one of light artillery were raised, while thirty redoubts were constructed on the frontier to keep back the Circassians. Cossack officers were sent by the Governor-General to finish their training in St. Petersburg and—a deft stroke of policy—Richelieu arranged that they should provide a squadron of Cossacks for the imperial guard. The warriors' rather muddled finances were next taken in hand and straightened out for them by their Governor, who also provided them with a hospital, a stud farm for horses, a model sheep pen for wool shearing and a factory for making it into uniform cloth ; while the school for the children of officers and men was enlarged to cope with the increase in population. The result of all these wise measures on the part of Richelieu was that out of a horde of disorganised bandits he fashioned a flourishing community of some 40,000 souls, who moreover were to provide Russia with her finest soldiers.

Richelieu was a disciple of Sully, for whose views he had a deep respect, and hence he thought little of manufactures except for objects of prime necessity ; he felt that it was of far more vital importance to cultivate the immense tracts of untilled land all over the three districts. He therefore believed agriculture to be one of the chief pillars of New-Russia, and he took the keenest interest in the quality of the grain produced, which he would himself examine in the shops. If he thought any of it not up to standard, he would not hesitate to rebuke the producer : " Take care ; they will not be pleased with this abroad, and you will do harm both to yourself and to us." He encouraged and gave protection to the raising of good breeds of sheep, so as to improve the quality of the wool, and as always he went about himself inspecting the herds. A German, Müller, introduced near Odessa merino sheep from Spain in 1804, and later on, the two daughters of a Marseilles merchant were to be found owning a flock of 35,000 merinos on the north-west of the Perekop isthmus. More than 200 Swiss families having come to settle in New-Russia in 1803, a native of Geneva, Pictet de Rochemont, set up a model sheep run on

his property at Novoï-Lancy, while another Swiss founded a
similar establishment on the left bank of the Bug.

Richelieu was the first to see the possibilities of vine culture
in the territory of New-Russia, and he considered it to be of
great importance. Vines were imported from France and
flourished exceedingly, so that French travellers, we are told,
were astonished to find wines so far from home with the
authentic flavour of Bordeaux and Burgundy. In the Perekop
isthmus, the duke turned his attention to the salt marshes ;
with improved methods, these were made to yield ten times
their previous output—to the great profit of the imperial
revenues. Since in seasons of heavy rain there would often
be a scarcity of salt, Richelieu caused storehouses to be opened
where a year's supply could be kept in store for such emer-
gencies. At Koslov, he revived the output of medicinal mud,
and at Nikita with his usual zeal for planting vegetation, he
created a botanical garden. Many other towns, including
Rostov, Taganrog and Ekaterinoslav, grew rapidly and prospered under the stimulus of his care. So too, did Kherson,
which during the reign of Catherine had been in a state of
decay. Richelieu caused a fine new quay to be constructed
along the banks of the Dnieper, which preserved the town
from stagnant flood water and its resulting evils.

If the prosperity of New-Russia was to derive primarily
from the products of her soil, the exportation of these products was equally important ; hence Richelieu's great interest
in and encouragement of merchants of all nations. Those of
New-Russia had frequent dealings with Constantinople and
the whole Asian coast from Smyrna to Alexandria, even with
Persia, India and Siberia ; they dealt also with Italy and
southern France, especially Marseilles, and under Richelieu's
encouragement, trade between Odessa and Marseilles took a
great bound forward.

In addition to all these aspects of his work, the Governor-
General of New-Russia was also Inspector-General of the
troops numbering about 40,000 men who were stationed
in the three districts, commanding-officer of the division

permanently garrisoned in Odessa and its neighbourhood, and in charge of three recruiting depôts, as well as other civil and military establishments. He had two aides-de-camp : the Russian Stempkowski, and his young cousin, Léon de Roche-chouart, whom he treated like a son and who was devoted to him. Besides these two, his personal entourage consisted of three staff officers and two engineer-officers, his chancellery of three or four chiefs of division and several secretarial assistants. Richelieu had no personal secretary, however ; he opened the post himself, received all petitions, noting down recommendations on them and annotating other important papers in his own hand. He wrote with great fluency without making any alterations, whether in Russian, French, German or English, and nearly always, we are told, while humming or even singing at the top of his voice, leaning on a tiny round table, where there was hardly sufficient room for his elbow ! In this curious position he would work for eight or ten hours a day, during the course of which he not only dealt with his official papers, and sent in each year a statistical report on his territories, but also found time to attend to an extensive personal correspondence. Nor did he fail to read all the gazettes and periodicals which came to him, for he was an avid reader; his bedside table was well supplied with books, amongst which were always to be found volumes of Virgil and Cicero.

Richelieu's mode of living was frugal and simple, as indeed it had to be, for he had nothing now but his salary to live on, plus a grace-and-favour allowance of 15,000 roubles a year from the Tsar. His bed was simply a couch in his study, upon which sheets were laid at night. He rose at six a.m. in summer and winter alike, took a cup of coffee at eight, gave audiences for an hour (except on Sundays and feast days), then worked until 12.30 with the three civil secretaries of the governments of Kherson, Ekaterinoslav and the Crimea. He dined at one o'clock ; about twenty people would usually sit down to table, fourteen of them being members of his own household and staff, his doctor Scudery, and the Abbé Labdan, the duke's former tutor. The Abbé had had a severe nervous breakdown on hearing of the execution of the Duc d'Enghien, another of his pupils, and Richelieu had received the poor old man into his house at Odessa and was taking care of him. The other persons present at dinner were usually foreign consuls, important personages who happened to be passing through Odessa, or merchants.

Living, says Léon de Rochechouart, was very cheap in Odessa. Butchers' meat was of very good quality, the Black Sea provided an abundance of fish, as the steppes did of game, and the Crimea of fruit and vegetables, though later on the Governor's establishment was able to provide its own garden produce. It would appear, however, that in spite of all this varied choice of food, no great imagination was shown in the planning of the duke's meals ; since Castelnau, who dined every day with Richelieu, could not refrain from asking the duke one day whether he would mind if some dish other than chops were to appear at table ; since, said the poor man, he had reached the stage when he felt he could no longer swallow them. " My dear fellow," replied the duke in the most genuine astonishment, " is it possible that I have been eating them every day for three years ? Really, I had not noticed it."

After dinner, Richelieu would either work again or go out until the evening. Supper, which was at nine p.m., was never such a large gathering ; but it was the duke's habit always to invite some of the prominent people of Odessa, who could then talk freely to him. During the summer, he did not usually work in the evenings, but would be out of doors, walking, inspecting, cultivating a little piece of land he possessed, or going out in society or to public entertainments. For in spite of his busy official life, Richelieu never failed to appear at any social functions, and these were many when his cousin Léon de Rochechouart set to work to liven up Odessa with such amenities as opera, ballet and balls.

Rochechouart in his memoirs gives us a picture of social life in Odessa during these years. He himself, as second aide-de-camp, had a strangely assorted variety of tasks : in addition to being in charge of the duke's household, he had also to supervise the work of improving Odessa with promenades and plantations and the administration of the Casino. During the winter of 1807–8, an opera house and ballroom were opened in Odessa, performances being given by Polish and Italian companies and by a *corps de ballet*. Two amateur theatrical companies were also formed, one French and one Italian, and as it happened that the entire wardrobe of the court theatre at St. Petersburg had just been renewed, a large stock of costumes still in good condition was passed on to Odessa for the benefit of the two amateur companies. The leading lady of the French one, the daughter of Marie Antoinette's hairdresser, Leonard, was a *couturière* in Odessa ; she ran her establishment with the aid of two other French girls, and all three, Rochechouart assures us, married extremely well. The ballroom, or Redoute, was the scene of many masked balls which were organised with the aid of the Italian members of the community. Rochechouart mentions one in particular, held on the evening of Shrove Tuesday, at which an original and effective spectacle was staged. At a given signal, two " magicians " on stilts entered the ballroom from opposite sides, while six pages clad in white and six in black unrolled a great carpet representing an immense chess-board. To the sound of fanfares, the doors were then thrown open, and through one of them entered a king and queen in black followed by a complete set of chess pieces also dressed in black. The whole procession arranged itself in the appropriate positions on the board, while a similar procession clad in white which had come through another door did likewise. The two magicians then played a living game of chess, by touching with their wands the pieces they desired to move. This performance was a triumphant success, since the Russians were particularly fond of chess.

During Richelieu's early years in Odessa, however, before all these social amenities were available, life must have been distinctly bleak and above all, intellectually arid. The duke's letters to his sister Armandine show how much he felt cut off from the world he had known. He writes to her in March

T.S.—6

1806 : " I have little consolation in the way of society or in the type of people among whom I live. I who was born to enjoy the pleasures of society . . . find myself absolutely isolated and deprived of all enjoyment of that kind." There was evidently some thought of Armandine coming out to her brother at Odessa, if her health could have stood up to the journey, as the Marquis de Montcalm was being particularly difficult at this time. Richelieu writes to his sister in April hoping that her health will improve sufficiently for her to come ; she will at least get some peace, he tells her, and will avoid entangling the Jumilhacs in a family quarrel.

On Sundays, Richelieu had as busy a day as on any during the week. In the early part of the morning, he would be " at home " to the local notables, and all who wished to see him could call ; it was, Sicard tells us, like a family reunion. The duke would then go off to hold a parade of his troops, after which he would visit the Gymnase to hear a conduct report on the pupils. Those who had done well would be taken out by him for the rest of the day; first of all to hear Mass, and then to dinner and an afternoon's amusement. But punctually at the appointed hour in the evening they would be returned to school. Sicard relates that at Kherson there was a military school for the children of soldiers which it was Richelieu's habit to visit at regular intervals. During his visits he had always found everything in the most perfect order, but he presently discovered from an indirect source that all this perfection was merely a show staged for his benefit. Without saying a word to anyone, he set out one day from Odessa and suddenly swooped down unexpectedly on the school, to find that what he had heard about it was only too true. Then and there he dismissed the directors, appointed in their place an officer of whose zeal and integrity he could be assured, and returned the following day to Odessa.

Sicard relates several anecdotes which throw a pleasing light on Richelieu's character. The duke, he said, never contracted a debt, and never even thought of borrowing from anyone in Odessa in spite of his very slender means. Yet if someone spoke of being hard up, or of wanting money for business, the duke would say, laughing : " Well, come to me, my coffers are open to you ; there are probably fifty roubles there, at your disposal." Indeed, says Sicard the Marseilles business man regretfully, Richelieu was sadly careless about money ; if he had anything at all, he would give it or lend it to the first person who asked him, and that without any proper security. " Since I have the money," he would say, " I lend it to you and beg you to return it to me because I am poor. But a formal deed is useless if you intend to repay me, and if you do not, it will certainly not be I who will force you to it." One day Sicard went to visit Richelieu at his country property, where the duke usually betook himself in the evenings during fine weather. " I was told that he was strolling in the neighbourhood and I found him sitting on a stone smoking his pipe, close to a house owned by Jews. He was talking to the master of the house and two or three peasants. ' I am fulfilling the duty of a good neighbour in visiting my neighbours,' said he, ' you have no idea what useful information I learn from these good people.' "

Léon de Rochechouart mentions how Richelieu, enchanted by the beauty of the Crimean coast, had for a long time dreamed of acquiring a little domain where he could go and relax, far from the troubles of Europe. At last his chance came when a rich Tartar landowner died without leaving any children. It appears that it was the habit of the Moslems on such occasions to band together, put up the money and divide the property among themselves, in order that it might not fall into the hands of Christians, whom they wished to keep away. On this occasion they were in fact preparing to take such action, when they discovered the identity of the prospective purchaser. Such was the affection and respect in which the duke was held, that by common consent they retired from the field, and left him to buy it for 4000 roubles, which was about 8000 francs. The property in itself consisted merely of an old ruin of a house set in a large garden with a little land attached. But it was superbly situated on the Black Sea coast, adjoining the village of Urzuov, with its old Genoese port. The ruined house was replaced by a villa in the Greek style, which in the eyes of the local Tartars was nothing short of a palace, while a German landscape gardener laid out the garden. At that period it seemed as if Richelieu and Rochechouart would be fated to spend the rest of their lives in Russia, and the duke said that he would leave Urzuov to Rochechouart in his will ; he jokingly christened his young cousin Urzuov-Aga. But the future held events which were to change the course of their lives, and the eventual inheritor of Richelieu's charming retreat was to be his Russian aide-de-camp, Colonel Stempkowski.

CHAPTER IV

WARS AND EXCURSIONS

After the signing of the Treaty of Jassy in 1792, there had been a period of peace between Russia and Turkey, chiefly because the French Revolution and its European repercussions had given the rulers of Russia more serious preoccupations. But when the Tsar Alexander came to the throne, he seemed inclined to revert to his grandmother's scheme for the breaking-up of the Ottoman Empire, and the Porte was greatly alarmed by fresh Russian activities : troop movements along the Dniester, the throwing of pontoons across the Danube, and, above all, Russian intrigue in the subject principalities of Moldavia and Wallachia. The two hospodars of these provinces were abruptly deposed by Turkey, and though in face of Russia's menacing attitude the Sultan subsequently climbed down and reinstated them, the Tsar affected to consider himself insulted. Although therefore the Russian ambassador at Constantinople was under the impression that the affair had been peacefully settled, Alexander ordered General Michelson to invade Upper Moldavia.

Michelson had in fact been spending the summer of 1806 touring the garrisons of New-Russia, for the ostensible purpose of a general inspection, in reality in order to confer with the Governor-General over plans for the occupation by Russia of Moldavia, Wallachia and Bessarabia. The army now set in motion was made up of three divisions, of which the first was commanded by Richelieu.

No official declaration of war having been made, the Turks were not expecting to fight, and the three commanders indeed hesitated to attack them. As for the Pashas shut up in the fortresses, they were without ammunition, adequate garrisons, or any news from Constantinople ; they therefore saw even less object in showing fight. In fact, those in charge of Bender and Jassy came forth to meet the Russian generals as if to welcome honoured guests. Richelieu, who had crossed the Dniester with his division of 4000 men, 600 horse and 12 guns, entered Akerman at the head of two companies of Grenadiers. Accompanied by only eight or ten men, he then went to pay a call on the governor, whom he found surrounded by a body-guard armed to the teeth. Drinking the cup of coffee which was politely offered to him, Richelieu carried on a conversa-tion until such time as he was informed that his own troops were drawn up outside the windows. He then announced pleasantly but firmly to the Pasha that the troops must be lodged by the townspeople. The Turks proved most accom-modating in doing all that was required of them—and more, since gifts were soon being exchanged between the com-manders of the opposing forces. The Pasha bestowed a fine Arab horse on Richelieu, while the duke returned the attention with a variety of gifts which included one hundred Dutch ducats, to be shared out amongst the Turkish officers. It is related that on one occasion while Richelieu was entertaining the Pasha of Akerman, among those present was the dragoman who had actually conducted the negotiations between Richelieu and the Pasha for the surrender of the town. The Pasha sent a message to the duke through a Turkish-speaking intermediary that he would be greatly obliged if Richelieu would have the dragoman's head cut off, as he had taken a dislike to the man. On the duke's replying that he was quite unable to oblige the Pasha in this manner, the Turk expressed the greatest astonish-ment that a Governor-General should have such limited powers.

After the surrender of Akerman, Richelieu's division pressed on southwards towards the Danube and took posses-sion of Kilia. They were now not far distant from Ismail, and Richelieu's troops were continuing their advance in that direction when the duke fell ill. For nearly three weeks his life appears to have been in real danger, and when he had sufficiently recovered to be moved he was obliged, at the end of 1806, to return to Odessa, leaving the command of his troops to his old comrade-in-arms Langeron, while the Marquis de Traversay took over provisionally the duties of Governor-General. In any case, the onset of winter in all its rigours had caused the Russians to call a halt to their operations. The whole of Bessarabia was now in their hands, and two army corps were stationed along the Pruth and the Danube to guard the territory which they were occupying.

By the spring of 1807, Richelieu had sufficiently recovered to set out on a visit to Jassy, the Moldavian capital, in response to an invitation brought to him by three boyars from that principality. With a suite of about a dozen people, which included his doctor and the devoted Léon de Rochechouart, he set out up the Dniester as far as Bender, then across Bessarabia into Moldavia, a pause being made to visit Trajan's wall before they actually entered Jassy. The Moldavian capital was the headquarters of the Russian troops who, says Rochechouart, still made war in the good old way by going into winter quarters and using the time there spent in reorganising their forces, before recommencing operations against the Turks. During this interval, time was whiled away with the usual round of balls, concerts and other festivities, in which the visitors joined with zest during the ensuing few weeks. Speaking of society in Jassy, Rochechouart says that the men, heavily bearded and clothed in the richest materials, crowned with fur caps and shod with Turkish slippers, had all the ponderous gravity of the Turks ; but that, anxious to appear civilised by European standards, they unwillingly accorded an unlimited amount of freedom to their women. The women did not fail to make the most of this freedom, following the latest fashions of Paris or Vienna, and trying to model themselves upon the great ladies of the *ancien regime* in France. Even their furniture came from Paris.

Before returning to Odessa, Richelieu had a great longing to revisit Ismail, the scene of his first trial of arms. The fortress was then being again blockaded, this time by General

Meyendorf with 10,000 men. Langeron was in command of a division on the right bank of the Danube and a flotilla of six chaloupes, upon the largest of which he had set up his headquarters. Richelieu's nephew, the Comte d'Aumont, was then serving under Langeron. But the young man was killed a short time afterwards, and Langeron wrote briefly of his death in a letter of July 1807 : " Richelieu is heartbroken ; his beloved adjutant, whom he brought up and looked upon as a son, has been killed in an attack I made on a battery." Richelieu and his party were spectators of operations against the island in front of the town. But the first reconnaissances were all repulsed, and as it became evident that the proceedings were going to be somewhat lengthy, the duke could not remain to see more, since the presence of the Governor-General of New-Russia was urgently required elsewhere.

For the Circassians had broken out again. Pausing only long enough in Odessa, therefore, to attend to the most urgent business, Richelieu set off at the head of his troops, crossed the Kuban river and advanced on Anapa, on the Black Sea coast. The signal for attack on the town was given by the ships of the supporting fleet from Sebastopol ; they opened up a heavy bombardment, in the midst of which two landing-parties launched attacks from the shore, while Richelieu charged with the cavalry from the land side. The three attacking columns penetrated the fortress simultaneously ; the attack seems to have taken the defenders by surprise and was completely successful, the duke setting up his head-quarters in the great mosque, which had escaped damage. Leaving a garrison in Anapa, Richelieu then returned to Odessa, though a number of small punitive expeditions were carried into the heart of the Caucasus, in an attempt to teach the Circassians the error of their ways. But the tough mountaineers were not easily to be tamed, and in 1809 a second large expedition had to be undertaken against them, under the command of General Rudzevitch, whose Cossacks spread such a trail of destruction, fire and wholesale massacre that the spirit even of the Circassians was broken and they sued for peace. What was yet more to the point was that they remained quiet for several years afterwards, during which time Richelieu offered them commerce in exchange for brigandage by establishing exchange marts at Anapa and Sudjuk-Kalé where the Circassians could trade their goods for salt, in which they were completely lacking. The Crown salt mines even advanced salt to merchants who wished to enter this trade. It occurred to Richelieu also that timber from the forests of the Caucasus would be of great value to Russia for naval construction. Finally by cultivating friendly relations with the Circassian chiefs, he was able to persuade them to send some of their children to the Gymnase in Odessa.

Meanwhile, in the spring of 1808, Richelieu had set out on a tour of his three government districts, commencing by an inspection of the German colonies round Odessa. These inspections entailed a considerable amount of travel, so that the Governor was sometimes absent from Odessa for as long as three months. But the greatest tax on his powers of endurance was probably the hospitality he received, especially at the hands of the Cossack chieftains. Rochechouart gives an amusing account of their visit to the Attaman of Catherinodar, who received them with all military honours and was most attentive in providing them with suitable lodging and sustenance. It was the latter which was to provide them with the sternest test of sheer physical endurance. " We remained at table for three hours, twice a day," says Rochechouart, " and in order not to offend the Attaman, we had to eat and drink heartily." What made the experience infinitely more gruelling was that each dish had to be served three times —three soups, three entrées, three roasts, three salads, and so on—" In honour of the Holy Trinity," the Attaman would tell his guests, " which I invoke at this moment." His words were instantly greeted by three salvoes of gunfire and three hurrahs roared by the assembled Cossacks. After a day of these Gargantuan meals, the guests were further obliged, before retiring to rest, to drink three glasses of tea and three of rum. However, the Attaman had apparently thrived exceedingly on this overpowering diet, the sheer immensity of which and his capacity for consuming it could only be appreciated, says Rochechouart, by those who had been present at these meals. He was, as one might indeed expect, a colossus of a man, some sixty years of age, though he looked no more than forty. In his youth he was said to have wrestled with an ox and to have overcome it. He had begotten a large progeny, of whose exact number he had long since lost count. Richelieu having asked, by way of making polite conversation, how many children the Attaman possessed, the giant turned to the Cossack who was waiting on him at table: "Trofimov, how many children have I?" "Eleven, General," was the answer. "And are they all boys?" pursued the duke, to cover up his attempts to smother the laughter which was threatening to choke him. "Trofimov," said the Attaman, again turning to the Cossack, "how many daughters have I?" "Four, General," was the answer, given with the most imperturbable calm.

It was at about this time that Richelieu was entrusted by the Tsar with the mission of provisioning the army in Moldavia. The sum of six million roubles in paper money was sent from St. Petersburg, the bundle, says Rochechouart, "forming a package three feet high, two feet long and two feet wide." It was deposited in the vaults of the Bank of Odessa. Quietly and at moderate prices Richelieu collected the necessary footstuffs, and when all was ready Rochechouart was sent to inform the commander-in-chief, who was by that time in Bucharest.

When war broke out between Russia and France in 1807, it brought its own problems to Odessa, where there were at least 1000 French subjects. Richelieu realised that their departure would be a grievous blow to the town, and he did not hesitate to put himself forward as a hostage for the good behaviour of his compatriots. He felt certain, he said, that those to whom he was rendering such a service would not compromise him by their actions. His confidence was not

misplaced, and Odessa was able to keep her French community. Moreover, it soon became apparent that the war
would not be altogether an ill wind for Odessa. By 1808, the
articles, particularly cotton goods, which Europe needed from
Turkey could no longer be brought by sea. An overland
route had therefore to be instituted from Smyrna across Asia
Minor up to the Sea of Marmora ; thence one part ran across
to Rodosto and through European Turkey to Vienna, the
other by ship up the Black Sea to Odessa, on the way to
Russian Poland, Austria and even France. This gave a
tremendous impetus to Odessa's trade, which was even
further increased when in the opposite direction merchandise
for Constantinople coming from Germany, France and Italy
began to flow through Odessa. Moreover the period of war
with Turkey did not produce the dislocation of Russian trade
which might have been supposed, for while Russian and
Turkish troops were fighting each other on the Danube,
merchants of the two nations did business together in the
Black Sea ports through the period 1806–12. This great trade
boom necessitated a great expansion of port facilities in
Odessa, especially of the quarantine station, and also gave
Richelieu the idea of setting up Chambers of Maritime Insur-
ance, nothing of which kind had previously existed in Russia,
even in St. Petersburg. The prosperity which Odessa was
enjoying at this time was also reflected in her social life ;
Rochechouart mentions the winter of 1808–9 as being a
particularly brilliant one, with a good company of Italian
players at the theatre, ballet at the Opera House, and a series
of balls at the Redoute with a plentiful selection of attractive
partners from Poland, Moldavia and Wallachia. The year
1808 was speeded to its exit in a whirl of gaiety.

But on the European horizon the storm clouds were piling
up darker and higher. As a result of attempts to try conclu-
sions with the master of an ever more unwilling Europe,
Austria, Prussia and Russia had been respectively laid on their
backs at Austerlitz, Jena and Friedland. The uneasy alliance
which Alexander had since concluded with the conqueror was

not working ; neither intended to become the instrument of the other. As Napoleon himself wrote to Eugène de Beau-harnais in May 1808 : "At bottom the great question is : who shall have Constantinople ? " Moreover, the Tsar's alliance with the enemy of Russia, ill received and misunder-stood by his own people, had placed a weapon for use against him into the hands of those who opposed his liberal reforms. In this difficult situation " There is no one in my wide dominions," he told Caulaincourt, " to whom I can open my heart." None except perhaps the one man who, as he was to tell La Ferronays in later years, could be relied upon to present to him the truth. In May 1809, he summoned Richelieu to St. Petersburg. The duke set out with Léon de Rochechouart, and in ten days and nights of travelling they covered the dis-tance of more than 1100 miles between Odessa and St. Petersburg. There is unfortunately no record of the con-versations which ensued between the Tsar and Richelieu, but it is certain that the latter would not have approved of Alexander's alliance with the upstart ruler of France, or have had any illusions as to the peril threatening Russia from that quarter.

In the Russian capital, Richelieu found many old friends and relatives, including his cousin, Count Charles de Rastignac. For to the annoyance of Napoleon, the Emperor Alexander was continuing to afford protection to a large number of French exiles ; among them was Count Joseph de Maistre, who as the diplomatic representative of the King of Sardinia spent fourteen years in St. Petersburg, where he wrote many of his works. Richelieu and Rochechouart, however, were able to remain only six weeks in the city—to the great regret of that gay social butterfly, Count Léon de Rochechouart—since by the end of that time the renewed outburst of the Circassians and other grave matters requiring Richelieu's attention compelled him to hurry back to Odessa as rapidly as so great a distance could be covered.

No sooner had the Circassians been ruthlessly dealt with by Rudzevitch's Cossacks than further serious trouble flared

TSAR ALEXANDER I
(Reproduced by gracious permission of Her Majesty the Queen)

up on the Black Sea coast near Anapa. This was to lead to a curious episode in Richelieu's career. He received a communication, worded in what appeared to him as offensively curt and peremptory language, ordering him to place several battalions of the troops under his command, including a regiment of Cossacks, at the disposal of the admiral in command of the Black Sea fleet. Richelieu was never able to trace the exact source of this order; it apparently emanated from the Ministry of War, possibly the work of some minor official seizing the opportunity to assert his own authority. But Richelieu, interpreting the incident not only as an affront to himself but as proof of a humiliating lack of confidence in his capabilities, brooded over the matter for some days and finally wrote a letter direct to the Tsar. Rochechouart was absent in Sebastopol at this time, but his account of the situation he found on his return gives us an illuminating picture of the duke's temperament.

"On my return from Sebastopol," he says, " M. de Richelieu did not breathe a word to me of the letter, but I found him unwell, even very changed, with his nerves all on edge as a result of being upset. Happily Dr. Scudery understood his constitution well and was devoted to him. He said to me : ' With the nervous temperament of our dear duke, one must replace the remedies which are powerless to cure his trouble with those that come from the heart, not the pharmacy.' In conjunction with the doctor, we soon got the better of his indisposition, which had taken the form of an obstinate nervous fever. We managed with some difficulty to get him over the acute crises which returned frequently, and which were aggravated by complete sleeplessness for twelve nights, accompanied by a refusal to touch any food. The cook triumphed over this difficulty by the preparation of a highly concentrated meat jelly ; sleep came with more reluctance, owing to the great irritation of the nerves. The least sound, even that of a clock pendulum, for instance, would exasperate him." Rochechouart tells how he finally got the duke to sleep by the ingenious device of dropping the voice gradually while reading to him, until it sank into the lowest and most soothing of monotones. "By this means, from the second day I managed to get him half an hour's sleep, which led to the first step forward. I continued thus for several days; each time sleep came more quickly and lasted longer."

The duke's final and complete cure was accomplished by the arrival of the Tsar's reply to Richelieu's letter. Alexander expressed his surprise and disapproval at the very idea of troops being used on an expedition without their commander having been consulted, and he assured the duke that such a thing was not likely to occur again. Finally, he was pleased to grant Richelieu's request for Rochechouart to be admitted to the Imperial Guard; the young man would be made a lieutenant of Chasseurs, which was the equivalent of a captaincy in a line regiment.

Peace was now completely restored, and the invalid's recovery was, we are told, the signal for great rejoicing. Obviously, the Governor-General had greatly endeared himself to the people for whom he had done so much, and his return to health was celebrated with even more social gaiety than usual, the duke himself taking his accustomed part in it. But it is clear that even these distractions and the other ceaseless activities of a busy life were not altogether able to dispel the inner sense of loneliness and separation from his family which his letters to his sister Armandine reveal. He writes to her at this time: "I greatly long to see you, I assure you, and when I think of the ground I cover every year about the countryside and that in a third part of that distance I could be at your side, I feel ready to set off at once. I must, however, take advantage of the first moment of peace we get in Europe to come to you, for this everlasting absence is unbearable. It is not that I am complaining of my stay here. On the contrary, there is no post that would suit me better in all respects, and if only my sister could be here with me, there would be absolutely nothing lacking." However, by 1810 a significant change had come over the scene. The cosmopolitan society of Odessa had been augmented by a number of Circassians, whose women have always been famed for their beauty, and Richelieu wrote to Mme de Montcalm that the women of Paris, lively as they were, would scarcely shine among these " really remarkable " beauties. But, he adds, she is not therefore to suppose that he has taken to himself a companion from amongst them, because " I will tell you in confidence that I have had for some time in my heart a very real and tender attachment which has made me quite my old self. Do not say a word about it, for I love mystery, even at 600 leagues." After which solitary gleam of revealing light, a discreet darkness descends again; even Armandine is not to know more.

In the following year, 1811, the Tsar's Polish mistress, Mme Narishkin, came south to Odessa with Sophia, the younger of the two daughters she had borne to Alexander; their elder daughter Zinaida having died the year before. Sophia was a pretty child, bearing a remarkable resemblance to her father, who idolised her; but like her sister she was not robust. In September, therefore, Mme Narishkin set out with her from Odessa on a trip to the Crimea for the benefit of Sophia's health, and they were escorted by the Governor-General and his staff, who evidently seized the opportunity of combining suitable attentions to Mme Narishkin with some of their periodical inspections. Kherson, Perekop, Batchi-Seraï and Sebastopol were all visited in turn, the great new naval base surpassing all the other towns with the splendour of its reception. After a review of the whole fleet, assembled and gaily beflagged in the harbour, the visitors were entertained to a dinner and ball at the Admiralty, and a performance of *Iphigenia* was given on the very place where according to ancient tradition the tragedy had been enacted. At Batchi-Seraï the party was entertained by whirling Dervishes, while the irrepressible Léon de Rochechouart, having disguised himself as a woman, succeeded in smuggling Mme Narishkin into the harem of a Moslem chieftain. However, in the midst of all these frivolities, Richelieu suddenly received orders to set about more serious business : he was to take possession of the port of Sudjuk-Kalé on the Black Sea, which the Turks had been quietly using as a port from which to supply the Circassians with ammunition. Madame Narishkin insisted on accompanying them as far as Anapa, where the expeditionary force was being assembled, and she travelled on horseback to visit the camp where Richelieu reviewed all the troops. After a ball in the evening, improvised in tents with military bands to provide the music, she departed the following day, enchanted with all that she had seen and done.

On the eve of setting off on his military expedition, Richelieu wrote to Mme de Montcalm that he was not expecting to be back in Odessa for six weeks, that he had, in fact, hardly spent two months in it during that year, and that he would have covered more than 5000 miles by the time he returned. " I lead the most vagabond life imaginable," he wrote, " but as it is the only means of doing any good in the immense new countryside which is entrusted to me, I take it in my stride. You are right, my dear, the one consolation in the position I am in is to be able to do some good, and that is all I care about."

When Richelieu and his force arrived at Sudjuk-Kalé, he found both the town and the fort abandoned. Nor was there any sign of the Russian fleet which should have been there to revictual his troops. This presently made its appearance, but there seemed no good reason for the delay in doing so, and Richelieu suspected that the real cause was a jealous unwillingness on the part of the naval force to support the army. While the Russians were occupying the empty fort, two Circassian princes appeared and suggested that there was a good opportunity of swooping down on and destroying the encampment of a powerful tribe in the neighbourhood. Richelieu acted upon this suggestion, but discovered that it was a trap when he suddenly found himself confronted with a force of more than 10,000 men. A desperate battle ensued, which resulted in the sanguinary repulse of the Circassians, who left 2000 of their men on the field. But the net result of the operations was as unproductive as all the previous expeditions against these warlike people. As Richelieu wrote to the Tsar, there would be no real settlement until peace had been made with the Turks, who were behind the Circassians, continually inciting them to fresh irruptions.

Richelieu had been working on Alexander for some time to make peace with the Porte, since he could see the day rapidly approaching when the Tsar would need every soldier he possessed to meet the menace which was looming up in the west. Moreover, a continuance of hostilities with Turkey was not going to do Odessa any good; the Turks were beginning to get difficult over entry to the Black Sea, and Odessa was already feeling the pinch of Napoleon's continental blockade. The Sultan, it seemed, was not indisposed to consider making peace; it was Russia who was blocking the way with her impossible demands, her anxiety to annex Moldavia and Wallachia, and certain points on the Caucasian coast. Richelieu wrote frankly to the Tsar that the Turks would never consider peace on such terms; that was as certain as the fact that the indefinite continuance of the war was holding down six Russian divisions and costing, in casualties from sickness alone, a third of the men employed. " This state of affairs," he wrote, " is bad enough now; what frightful consequences would it not entail if you were attacked from across the Vistula ? One cannot think of it without shuddering. . . . In God's name, Sire, deign to listen to the voice of a faithful servant who is deeply devoted to you. Perhaps, alas ! it will soon be too late. To-day you can have the Sereth ; who knows if, in another two years, you will be able to defend the Dniester ? All your resources will not be too many to repulse the storm which is menacing you ; gather them together, Sire, and let your flanks be free, while you fight on your front." Several times, Richelieu returned to the charge as his pleadings remained without result ; but in November 1811 the tide of war was running against Russia when the Turks forced the passage of the Danube, and he hastened to warn the Tsar that the moment was not now

favourable for negotiations, that they must wait until either
the rains or the imperial armies had forced the Turks back
again across the Danube. However, by the spring of 1812,
the sky had become so darkened with the ominous storm
clouds gathering in the west that the Tsar was at last goaded
to take action, though not before Richelieu had again been
summoned to a conference at St. Petersburg, where discussions continued for a fortnight with the Tsar and his
ministers. Peace was at last to be made with Turkey, the
opportunity having been most conveniently presented through
the ineptitude of the Grand Vizier who had allowed himself to
be surrounded in an indefensible position by Russian troops.
A treaty was therefore agreed upon and signed at Bucharest in
May. There was no question now of retaining Moldavia and
Wallachia. They were a small price to pay for the purchase of
Turkish neutrality in the coming struggle of the giants, a price
which was paid not a moment too soon. Yet the Tsar was
determined that the conflict should not be precipitated by any
offensive action on his part. " I shall not break the peace ; "
he told Napoleon's representative, General Lauriston, " if
your master wishes to find me, he must come to seek me, for
I shall not advance to meet him."

Richelieu, however, was ordered to direct all his available
troops to Volhynia in Russian Poland. The Tsar also wrote
to him invoking his protection for Mme Narishkin and
Sophia, asking him, if the worst happened and the Russian
armies were forced to retreat from New-Russia, to help the
mother and child to make their escape into the interior of the
country. The provinces of New-Russia were practically
denuded of troops, only a skeleton force of convalescents and
recruits being left to man the Caucasian frontier ; but it was
hoped that this would now remain quiescent for some while
to come, especially as peace had been made with Turkey. But
many of the garrison towns of New-Russia were a long distance away from Volhynia, and in spite of forced marches
some of the regiments were unable to reach their destination
until after war had actually begun. For on the night of 23rd-

24th June the Tsar sent Richelieu a dramatic message from Vilna : " Hostilities have commenced, my dear General. Napoleon, without any explanation or preamble whatever, has attacked us at Kovno." While the French army was crossing the Niemen, the Tsar was attending a ball he was giving to the Polish nobility at Zakret, little more than twenty miles away. When the news of the invasion was brought to him, however, he did not reveal it to those present, but continued to move about among his guests with an appearance of unruffled calm. Yet on returning afterwards to his headquarters he spent the remainder of the night composing a manifesto in which he declared his determination not to lay down his arms while a single enemy soldier remained on Russian soil.

As for Richelieu, he was keenly anxious to go to the front at the head of his troops. In his detestation of the man whom he always referred to either as " the Usurper " or as " Buonaparte," he wrote to the Tsar : " May I not have the pain of remaining inactive in this struggle of the Spirit of Good against the Spirit of Evil ! May God protect you in this just cause, which is of concern to all thinking people ; it is that of the liberty of the world against the Usurper, of humanity against tyranny. May you be destined by providence to arrest this torrent of evils ! " He informed the Tsar that he was calling in all troops spread out over the territories of New-Russia, that when they had been assembled into an army corps he asked to have the command, since he would be inconsolable if the troops he had raised were to fight without him. His next action was to assemble the notables of Odessa and urge them to show themselves true Russians in this time of national emergency ; there could be, he told them, no more flattering reward to himself for all that he had done and would do for his new country. He set an example by giving to the Treasury the sum of 40,000 roubles. He then began to make preparations for taking up command of his troops and setting forth to join the army corps of General Tomasov in Volhynia.

But fate, in a sinister and unforeseen guise, was about to thwart all his plans.

CHAPTER V

THE VALLEY OF THE SHADOW

On the 12th August 1812, one of the dancers at the Odessa theatre died suddenly after only thirty-six hours' illness. While the doctors were puzzling over her symptoms, another and yet a third dancer was taken ill and shared her fate. Richelieu then began to make some enquiries which revealed the disquieting fact that there had been recently a decidedly larger number of sudden deaths than usual in Odessa. Here was something that required looking into. He divided the town into twelve districts, each under the control of a responsible inhabitant assisted by a doctor, and a committee was set up consisting of these men and the doctors, the Chief of Police and other officials, with Richelieu himself as President. The committee held its first meeting on the 21st August, and the evidence produced confirmed that there had been and was continuing to be an unusually sharp rise in the death rate. But the doctors, who seem to have been remarkably dim even by the not very bright medical standards of those days, were still unable to agree about the cause of the deaths, which were variously ascribed to " a malign fever," " over-indulgence in spirituous beverages," or in the case of the dancers, to an even less polite cause. Alone among his colleagues, the doctor in charge of the quarantine station uncompromisingly pronounced the dread word plague.

Although the main gateway of Odessa's trade was Constantinople, the Russian ambassador there had not thought it necessary to warn the health authorities in Odessa that plague was raging in the Ottoman capital, where it had appeared in the previous year for the first time since the days of the French expedition to Egypt. No doubt the relatively small number of people who had died in Odessa was considered of little significance compared to the 2000 who were dying of plague in a single day in Constantinople. Even though the rise in Odessa's death rate was found subsequently to have been going on for at least the previous six weeks, the local doctors had remained blissfully unaware of the true cause, which seems to have originated in the arrival in the port of Odessa of an Austrian ship from Constantinople whose crew bribed the quarantine authorities to let them go ashore although several of their number had died during the voyage.

Richelieu's first impulse was simply to isolate the town. But on second thoughts he realised that this alone would be of little avail, since cases were soon being reported from the countryside. He therefore caused the isolation line to be extended to the river Bug on one hand, and the Dniester on the other, the zones joining at 100 versts from Odessa. In the town itself, all public places not in urgent use were closed, while the two schools were put into quarantine. Each district was inspected twice daily by its commissar, who laid his report before the committee, which met each morning in the open air. In view of the late season of the year, Richelieu formed another committee to ensure that adequate food supplies were laid in for the coming winter, and—equally important—to prevent black marketing.

It was, however, not easy to maintain strict quarantine and isolation measures in a town with such a heterogeneous population as Odessa, especially among the poorer elements. In spite of all the precautions taken, the sinister invader's grip tightened upon the town. There could be no question now of the Governor going off to the war against the enemy who had by then occupied Moscow; in Odessa there was, literally, a war to the death with an enemy close at hand and infinitely more deadly. Richelieu, therefore, considering that his first duty was to the people of Odessa and of all New-Russia in their hour of trial, arranged for a deputy to take over provisionally the command of his troops, sent off Léon de Rochechouart to the front, and himself prepared to come to grips with the enemy at home.

On the 22nd November, a state of general quarantine was declared in the town. This meant that the doors of all houses were closed and no one was permitted to go out, or even appear on the threshold of a house, unless he were connected with the public services, in which case he would be provided with a special pass. Two Cossack horsemen patrolled each street in opposite directions to see that this regulation was enforced. The commissar of each district arranged for food to be brought round to the beleaguered inhabitants twice a day under police escort, and the money paid for it was received in a basin of vinegar. The food itself was swilled in cold water, bread being fumigated. Letters were also fumigated before distribution and then handed to the recipient on the end of a stick; after receipt they were fumigated a second time. Odessa under these conditions presented a scene of melancholy desolation comparable with London in 1665. With the suspension of all civic life, a deathly silence reigned in the streets, and Richelieu could not help confiding to one of the commissars how much it wrung his heart to be obliged to reduce to this condition the very streets which he had laboured for ten years to fill and animate. The mournful silence of the streets was broken only by the sound of the patrols and of certain carts carrying lights of a shuddering significance : those with a red flame, transporting stricken victims to hospital, those with a dark flame indicating victims beyond human care. Each morning, Richelieu would set out with his friends and compatriots the Abbé Nicolle and the Chevalier de Rosset ; clad in tarred overalls, they superintended the distribution of provisions to the hospitals and infected quarters of the town, the actual work being performed by convicts who had been promised their liberty if they survived. In the evening they would return for sea baths and a change of clothes, after which they went off again to superintend the removal and burial of the dead. On one occasion, as they were passing a plague-stricken house, a dying woman dragged herself to the door and thrust into Richelieu's arms a young child which she begged him to take into his care. In a stricken village where such terror reigned that the dead were lying unburied, the duke himself took a spade and set to work in order to shame the grave-diggers into activity.

In the midst of so much death and suffering, Richelieu's thoughts began to turn towards religion, away from the eighteenth-century scepticism in which he, like most of his generation, had grown up. The Abbé Nicolle, who by this time had become one of the duke's closest friends, was over-joyed to see such signs of awakening, and he relates how, after being able to set at rest one or two doubts in the duke's mind, he received his confession and with his own hands gave him communion in the catholic church at Odessa.

At last with the dawn of a new year, it seemed that the long nightmare of plague was coming to an end. On the 7th January 1813, after sixty-six days of complete seclusion, Odessa was declared open once more. The visitation had cost the lives of some 3000 of her citizens, a number not inconsiderable for a town the size of Odessa, and which would probably have been a great deal larger but for the Governor's stringent pre-cautions. Now that the hideous burden was lifting from his shoulders, however, Richelieu could not help longing to get away from the scene of horror in which he had been imprisoned while such stirring events were happening elsewhere. Once more his thoughts began to turn to the war, in which the Russian armies were by this time pursuing the broken remnants of the invaders across Germany. He wrote to the Tsar in February, asking that he might now be permitted to go and serve in the army, even if only as an ordinary soldier. It was not ambition, he said ; he realised that it was too late in the day for him to be able to distinguish himself in the campaign ; he wished only to show his goodwill, and " I will also confess to you, with the confidence inspired by your former kindnesses, that I would like to get out of this hell and be reborn into life a little." He pointed out that if, with the coming of spring, there should happen to be any recurrence of infection, all measures were now organised to cope with it, and they should be continued into the summer. To Rochechouart he wrote at the same time, speaking of this appeal to the Emperor, saying that he had made quite enough sacrifices by remaining in Odessa and that permission to rejoin Rochechouart was the one thing which could console him for what he had suffered.

But if plague had been stamped out in Odessa, it had not left New-Russia. In July, Richelieu was writing to Rochechouart that by some " inexplicable fatality " it had reared its head in Elizabethgrad, though Richelieu by hurrying there and taking prompt measures had succeeded in stamping it out again. He was now in better spirits, telling Rochechouart that he had become quite an expert in matters of plague and that he actually feared it less than some of the disastrous measures taken by the authorities to prevent it, which were merely killing the prosperity of the country. He added, in more cheerful vein, that he was living in a house in the country filled with flowers and fruit. A month later, he wrote again to Rochechouart that although there had been no fresh outbreak of plague in Odessa that summer, it still kept cropping up in odd villages about the countryside, which kept him travelling about exercising his talent for fighting plague—*c'est toujours un joli talent de société.*"

All these happenings made Richelieu realise the inadequacy and inefficiency of the existing health regulations and facilities. He therefore submitted to the Minister of the Interior a series of suggestions for reforms. But he was battering his head vainly against the brick wall of Russian bureaucracy : the government continued to maintain the old quarantine and sanitary regulations long after the plague had disappeared, when their sole effect was to strangle the trade and prosperity of the countryside. The worst offender in this respect appears to have been the Governor-General of Little-Russia, Prince Alexis Kurakin. The territories of Little-Russia, which included the Ukraine, were the chief channel through which grain and other commodities came down from the north to the port of Odessa for shipment further afield. Yet Odessa's trade, and hence her recovery, was being strangled by emergency measures which were still being rigorously applied long after the emergency itself had ceased to exist. Richelieu wrote in desperation to Prince Alexis Kurakin in May 1813 that in view of the state of distress existing in Odessa and its neighbourhood, the emergency measures, if not relaxed, could only result in the complete ruin of the whole countryside. For five months now, he said, there had been no case of plague ; spring had come two months since, and if there had been any germs lurking anywhere, they ought to have developed. Even the celebrations at Easter, when people crowd together and bring out belongings which have been stored away, did not result in the occurrence of a single case of plague. He urgently entreated the Prince to restore free communication between towns and villages, raise the cordon which shut off Odessa and let them keep the existing line on the Bug without demanding the setting-up of more posts from the unfortunate Cossacks who, out of a population of little more than 6000 males, had 2000 of them away on service. As for the Black Sea and Sea of Azov, where navigation was still absolutely forbidden, surely this regulation could now be relaxed if the same precautions were taken as for ships coming from Constantinople ? It is to be feared, however, that Richelieu's pleas fell on deaf ears, for in December the Spanish Consul at Odessa was writing to Rochechouart : " We are delivered, thank Heaven, from the plague, but there still remains for us an even greater scourge, Prince Kurakin, Governor-General of Little-Russia. You can have no idea of all the eccentricities and vexations which come from this great man ; his memory will last much longer in this countryside than the plague." As for Richelieu, " the good duke," it is only his philosophical nature and his love of the public welfare which enables him to support all these trials, says the Spaniard.

However, at about this time a little light relief was brought to the scene by the arrival in Odessa, on her long journey to Vienna, of Queen Marie-Caroline of Naples. Her tempestuous majesty arrived after a particularly unpleasant voyage from Constantinople across the Black Sea which was in one of its most refractory moods, and her ruffled nerves were far from being soothed on finding that she had to go into quarantine like other travellers. Nor was she any better pleased when after remaining there twenty-seven days, which was the time set by the Odessa authorities, an overriding order came, rather typically, from St. Petersburg to the effect that she must remain in quarantine for another fifteen days. The daily visits of Richelieu, however, did much to sooth her outraged feelings, and when at last she emerged from seclusion on the 14th December, she was entertained with all that Odessa had to offer in the way of plays and operas before she resumed her journey. She set forth again on the 18th, escorted by Richelieu, who travelled with the party as far as Tulczyn, just over the Polish border. Here she was received with medieval splendour by Count Felix Potocki's widow, who in her youth had been the guest of the Queen's sister Marie-Antoinette at Versailles. At this point Richelieu left the royal traveller in charge of Count Armand de Saint-Priest who as Governor of Podolia took over escort of the party, while Richelieu returned to Odessa.

So the year 1813 slipped away, and as it drew to its close the former master of Europe, in his retreat from the blood-soaked field of Leipsic, reached the Rhine with such remnants of his newly raised forces as had not shared the fate of their brothers of the Grand Army. Now he was fighting a rearguard action, while the Allies closed in upon him. France was being invaded ; Russia, Austria and Prussia were advancing on Paris, while in the south Wellington was driving Soult before him towards Bayonne. But no release came yet for the Governor of Odessa, and in March 1814 Richelieu was expressing his frustration in a letter to Rochechouart : " What would I not give for the Emperor to call me to his side ? Alas, he used to wish me well, I used to believe that he even felt friendship for me. . . . He must have completely forgotten me, for I feel that I have done nothing which could make me undeserving of the kindnesses he used to show me."

In the meantime Richelieu continued his struggle to save the commercial life of the town from the throttling stranglehold of officialdom. He wrote direct to the Minister of Finance that the harvest of 1813 had almost completely failed ; that in spite of the ravages of plague in the districts of Kherson and the Crimea, no help had been received from the government. On the contrary, all the usual taxes were being relentlessly collected, even including arrears. The result was that the workhouse at Kherson was filled with unfortunates unable to pay, who had, after all, to be supported by the Treasury. Richelieu suggested that under these exceptional circumstances the only real remedy would be to grant exemption from taxes for three years, with the remittance of arrears. He also wrote to the Tsar pleading for an alleviation of certain customs duties in favour of Odessa. Russia, he said, ought to do everything possible to attract the trade of the East, for which at present Smyrna was the outlet. But Sinope could be an even better one, he pointed out, since it was actually on the Black Sea, and if it were linked directly with Odessa, the latter would become the gateway for all the trade between Europe and the East. But in opening up a new trade route, one must always offer some advantage, and this could be done by granting a preferential customs rate for Eastern products shipped between Sinope and Odessa. As for his colleague of Little-Russia, not only were Richelieu's frequent appeals unheeded, but Prince Kurakin had even surpassed himself by bringing in yet more stringent regulations ; in fact, his precautions grew in inverse proportion as the necessity for them receded. In June, Richelieu wrote to him that his new requirements for the disinfection of merchandise would be the final ruin of Odessa. How was it going to be possible, the duke demanded, to purify cotton goods with muriatic acid in the huge airy warehouses such as those of Odessa and all the other quarantine stations of the world ? They would have to start by rebuilding them. It was unfortunate, added Richelieu tartly, that since His Excellency had been inhabiting the region, he had not once paid a visit to this part of it.

In June, too, he wrote again to Rochechouart about the matter that was nearest his heart : " As soon as the Emperor returns to Russia, I shall ask to go and see him in St. Petersburg and obtain the leave I need to go to Paris. I am astonished that he did not accord it to me at my family's request, for he must want to talk over with me many matters concerning this country, and for my part I would like to see him for the same reason." Another three months were to pass by in anxious expectation, but at last in September came the long-awaited permission to move. On the 26th September, Richelieu set out from Odessa, and Charles Sicard has left us an account of the scenes which attended the duke's departure. " A large part of the population accompanied him outside the town, showering blessings and good wishes on him. More than 200 persons followed him as far as the first posting station, where a farewell banquet had been prepared." Richelieu's health was drunk, with best wishes for a good journey and his safe return ; loud cheers echoed over the steppes, but they were suddenly stifled by sobs, as though those present had a sudden presentiment that they would never see him again. As the duke prepared to go to the waiting carriage, people crowded round him, embracing him, kissing his hands and even the skirts of his coat. All were deeply moved, and the duke himself dissolved in tears, saying " My friends, spare me this scene." He was picked up bodily and carried shoulder high to his carriage. So he departed, from the places and people who, as indeed it turned out, were never to see him again : from the flourishing city port of 40,000 people which he had fashioned out of a poor little town of barely 8000 inhabitants without trade or amenities ; from the provinces of New-Russia, transformed from uncultivated desert peopled by nomad tribes into a rich countryside become one of the granaries of Europe, with a population increased by a million souls ; from the Crimea, a garden luxuriating with vines and dotted with elegant villas, where he himself had his little domain of Ursuov. A Russian, Muravief Apostol, visited Ursuov a few years later and has left a touching account of the affectionate memory in which Richelieu was still held by the Tartar inhabitants of that neighbourhood, who had not ceased to long for his return and anxiously enquired for news of him; since, as the village head-man assured their Russian visitor, they looked upon Richelieu as a father.

It was not to St. Petersburg that the duke had been sum-moned by the Tsar, but to Vienna, where the allied sovereigns and their ministers were gathering for the opening of the famous congress which was to remake the map of Europe. From Vienna, Richelieu wrote to Mme de Montcalm that, glad as he was to be on his way to his family, he would much have preferred to have gone first to St. Petersburg, so that he could have given a proper detailed account of his administra-tion and of the management of the enormous sums of money with which he had had to deal. He did not wish, he said, to leave the country without giving this account of his steward-ship ; it was intolerable to him that anyone should be able to think that he had seized the opportunity to decamp at that moment and so evade responsibility. Nevertheless he did have the opportunity of having a long talk with the Tsar in Vienna about the affairs of Odessa, and he pressed once more upon Alexander the idea of making the town a free port. Richelieu had long favoured this course, which he assured the Tsar would be the only real way to develop the commerce of the Crimea and prevent the smuggling which was only too often the true source of epidemics. He also obtained the Tsar's approval for his scheme for transforming the Institute of Odessa into a Lycée, which was to bear his own name.

Finally, from Vienna, Richelieu also wrote to Léon de Rochechouart, now back in Paris, informing his cousin that the Tsar was giving him temporary leave to revisit France in order to see his family and pay his respects to the King. He begged Rochechouart to hand to Louis XVIII a letter in which he set forth the reasons which had prevented him from appear-ing sooner and from taking up again his post of First Gentle-man of the Bedchamber. These proprieties having been duly observed, Richelieu then started in November 1814 on the journey to France, across whose frontiers he had not set foot for twelve eventful years.

PART THREE

PRIME MINISTER

CHAPTER I

PRELUDE

At the end of November 1814, Richelieu arrived in Paris. He had asked Léon de Rochechouart to find him a suitable lodging, but his cousin insisted that the duke should join him in the furnished apartment which he had rented from Baron Louis in the Rue Royale. The King had meanwhile sent messages of goodwill through Rochechouart, expressing his pleasure at the duke's return and the satisfaction he would feel at having Richelieu's presence in the royal councils.

But it is clear enough that at this time Richelieu had no intention of remaining in France, or of taking up again permanently his post of First Gentleman of the Bedchamber. It would indeed have been impossible for him to do so while he remained in the service of the Tsar, as it was equally impossible for him to quit that service abruptly, after all the kindness which Alexander had shown him. Richelieu's purpose in returning to France was the very natural one of wishing to arrange a final settlement of his own affairs after all the years of turmoil, to see his family, and to make sure that they were as well provided for as was possible with the means remaining at his disposal. There was little enough remaining for them from the wreck of the family fortunes ; the Richelieu estate had been broken up in 1805 and sold in lots. Napoleon had thought at one time of bestowing the château on one of his marshals, but it was already so dilapidated that the cost of repairing it would have been prohibitive, and although the ruined shell of the building, bereft of all its valuable contents, now returned to the family, it was more of a liability than an asset, in view of their financial position. The duke wrote to Langeron, who was acting in his place as Governor of Odessa, that as far as money was concerned, he had " nothing to expect from France ; even my statues and pictures, according to the law, can neither be returned to me nor paid for ; as for land, I do not possess the width of an *ecu*. This is rather sad above all for my sisters, who are very poor ; as for me, provided that France is happy, I shall not have the least regret." A few days later he was writing again to Langeron that although his pictures and statues were now decorating the galleries of the Louvre, without his being able to claim any compensation— " such is the law, to which I submit without complaint "— he had, after all, been able to retrieve about 36,000 francs out of the wreckage of the family fortunes. He had given this sum to his sisters : " They were far from being opulent and this trifle will not enrich them very much ; but at least if either of them wants to go out, she will be able to do so in a carriage, which they have been unable to do up to now." As both of his sisters were by this time hunchbacks, and Mme de Montcalm, the elder one, was an invalid who spent most of her life on a couch, this improvement in their financial condition was no mere luxury.

After having devoted the first few days after his arrival to seeing those members of his family who were in Paris, there now remained for Richelieu to face the slightly embarrasing ordeal of paying a visit to Courteilles. His wife and mother-in-law had been living there ever since the painful episode of his marriage, and it was now twelve years since he had last seen them. He insisted on having the support of Léon de Rochechouart, who gladly accompanied him when they went there about the middle of December. The visit seems after all to have passed off very well, and the two men remained there until the New Year, when the Court ceremonies of New Year's Day obliged them to return to Paris in order to pay their respects to the King.

It was on one evening during this winter of 1814–15 that Mme de Boigne, as she relates in her memoirs, on paying her first visit to the *salon* of Mme de Duras, " saw a tall man come in with a handsome face, the youth of which contrasted

strangely with his grey hair.   He was very short sighted, and
was continually blinking in an unpleasing manner.   He wore
boots and was badly dressed to the point of affectation.   Yet
in spite of his attire, he preserved the manner of a *grand
seigneur*.   He threw himself upon a sofa and talked in a sharp
and high-pitched voice ; a slight foreign accent and somewhat
unusual turns of speech made me think that he was not a
Frenchman ; yet his language and above all the sentiments
which he expressed, refuted this idea.   I saw that he was on
familiar terms with all my friends, and I racked my brain to
conjecture who this well-known stranger might be : it was
the Duc de Richelieu, who had returned to France. . . . The
impression which he made upon me at this first meeting has
never changed." Mme de Boigne has to admit that Richelieu's
" fine and noble character, and his real business capacity,
together with his enlightened patriotism, commanded my
support, I might almost say my devotion ; but it was an
appreciation based on esteem rather than on liking." The
undertone of hostility which permeates all her references to
the duke, and her complaints of his " acrimonious manner "
probably have their roots in an incident which occurred later
on, when a plot was thought to be hatching against the government and a letter addressed to Fouché, then in Belgium, fel
into the hands of the Royalists.   Knowing Fouché, they felt
that it might well contain valuable evidence, and as the King
had gone out for his usual drive, Mme de Boigne and her
friends were persuaded to take the letter to Richelieu with the
suggestion that it should be surreptitiously opened.   From
what we have seen of the duke's character, however, it is not
difficult to imagine his disgust at the idea of such a proceeding,
whatever the end in view.   He received the deputation, Mme
de Boigne informs us, in the coldest manner and said that he
knew of no one under him who was either in the habit or
capable of opening letters.   He then tried to hand the letter
back to her ; she refused to take it, and they " separated in a
state of mutual vexation." The letter eventually reached the
hands of Decazes, who as Minister of Police had no such

scruples about opening other people's correspondence, and who, according to Mme de Boigne, personally thanked her for her action. But after her unfortunate encounter with Richelieu, although they met almost daily, each avoided the other and she says that they never again exchanged a word.

Meanwhile, the political situation in France was steadily deteriorating. The restoration of the old dynasty in the spring of 1814 had been accepted, if grudgingly, by the heirs of the Revolution, in the hope that it would at least bring an era of peace after the twenty-five years of war and despotism which had bled France white ; what she needed above all things was a period of rest and recovery. After the fall of Napoleon, nobody had seriously proposed setting up a republic ; there were too many people still alive for whom the word " republic " meant the Terror, a nightmare best forgotten. Even the die-hard republicans therefore found it expedient to mask their true sentiments for the time being and to profess instead a willingness for a constitutional sovereign who could be set up as a convenient figure-head to please the allied Powers, at least for so long as the troops of those Powers remained on French territory. For this purpose, Louis XVIII had served well enough, though they mistrusted his entourage. For the rest of the royal family they had only the deepest contempt. As for the Bonapartists, the discontented soldiers of the Empire met in the *salons* of the ex-Queen of Holland, Hortense de Beauharnais, and others of the same ilk, to lament the glorious days that had gone ; while Madame de Staël entertained such well-known firebrands as Benjamin Constant and Lafayette in enjoyable denunciations of the shortcomings of the government. The sudden release of the Press from the iron hand of the Napoleonic censorship to the freedom of speech customary under a constitutional monarchy had also given a tremendous stimulus to political discussion ; though the spiteful attacks on ministers, *émigrés* and clergy by such left-wing journals as the *Nain Jaune* were probably not as damaging to the monarchy in the long run as the violence of the royalist press, with its denunciation of everything connected

CHARLES PHILIPPE, COMTE D'ARTOIS (MONSIEUR)

with the Revolution and its openly expressed contempt for
the Charter of the new monarchy. A contemporary writer,
Duvergier de Hauranne, speaks of the impossibility of understanding Restoration politics without an appreciation of the
fundamental antipathy between the old France and the new.
To the Royalists, every so-called Liberal was a revolutionary
conspirator; to the Liberals, every Royalist was an enemy both
of the Revolution and of the Charter.

Unfortunately the Bourbons themselves could contribute
nothing towards cementing over these deep fissures in the
national fabric. To a large proportion of the population, they
had returned as complete strangers after an absence from
France of nearly a quarter of a century, and the figure of a
stout, infirm and elderly monarch, still wearing powdered hair
and the uniform of other days, was not calculated to stir the
nation to enthusiasm. Though his brother, the Comte
d'Artois, was, alone of his family, a fine figure of a man with
considerable charm of manner, he was also unfortunately the
one of whom it could most truly be said that he had learnt
nothing and forgotten nothing. Indeed it was his fatuous
boast that he and Lafayette were the only two men who had
not changed their views since 1789. Naturally therefore he
had gathered round him all the most intransigeant Royalists,
who made no secret of their contempt for the Charter and
their determination to work for the restoration of their old
privileges. As for the King, however much inclination he
might have to rule as a constitutional monarch, the " grey
eminence " who had the royal ear was the reactionary Ultra-
Royalist, Blacas, as much a stranger to the new France as his
master.

Further fuel was added to the smouldering political embers
by the tactless treatment of imperial veterans, particularly of
the Napoleonic marshals and their wives, who when they
appeared at Court were never allowed by the old nobility to
forget their origin. Nor, unfortunately, did the royal family
set a good example in this respect. Although the Duchesse
d'Angoulême may have been, as Napoleon said, the only man

among the Bourbons, she had inherited her father's *gaucherie* and her mother's pride, without any of Marie-Antoinette's charm.   The wife of Marshal Ney was the daughter of one of the late queen's most devoted personal maids, but the Duchesse d'Angoulême was quite unable on that account to display any graciousness towards her ; on the contrary, it is said that the treatment accorded to his wife, rankling in the mind of Marshal Ney, was one of the factors which was to cost the Bourbons his allegiance at the most crucial moment of the Hundred Days.

Meanwhile, in a letter to the Abbé Nicolle, Richelieu was unburdening himself of his impressions of the French nation after an absence of twenty-five years : " The national character is entirely changed ; the nation has developed rough, coarse manners which it never had before.   Religious feeling could scarcely be more feeble or more rare.   The upper classes think of nothing but to push themselves forward, to enrich themselves, to get good jobs ; all means are permissible to achieve that end.   You would be astounded if I told you details of what can be seen happening every day.   Bureaucracy is ten times worse than in Russia ; more than 10,000 letters a day are received in the various ministries.   I have yet to meet anyone who does not consider himself capable of filling any place in the administration—provided always that it is lucrative, and nearly all of them are.   The Ministry of the Interior alone costs ninety millions ; never was there a more costly administration."   Yet he has to make the depressing admission that this state of affairs was one which could not easily be altered without making a number of malcontents.

The Duke of Wellington had been in Paris as British ambassador since the end of August, but in view of the alarming accounts which were reaching the British Cabinet of the state of affairs in France, they began to feel very uneasy at leaving him in a position where, in the event of serious trouble, he might be seized as a hostage, even if no worse fate befell him.   In November, therefore, spurred on by a particularly grave report from Major-General Macaulay, Lord Liverpool,

the Prime Minister, began to press very strongly on Wellington
the desirability of his leaving the French capital. Macaulay
had pointed out that " the King of France's government is
notoriously weak, disunited and unpopular " ; that there was
a great deal of disaffection amongst soldiers, unemployed men
and " Jacobins," which he considered to be moving " in its
natural progress towards an explosion." The duke himself,
while agreeing about the desirability in principle of his being
moved from a place where he might be seized and immobilised
at the very moment when his services would be most needed,
yet maintained that from the point of view both of Anglo-
French relations and of his own reputation (" I must say I feel
my own character a little concerned in this transaction "), he
could only go when a suitable reason could be produced to
explain his departure. In December an eminently satisfactory
reason did in fact present itself when Lord Castlereagh, the
British Foreign Secretary, found it necessary for reasons of
domestic party politics to leave the Congress of Vienna and
return to England in time for the re-opening of Parliament.
Since Wellington was obviously the most fitting person to fill
such an important position at Vienna, the duke was able with
perfect propriety to make a strategic withdrawal from Paris—
a circumstance which in less than two months' time was to
prove a singularly fortunate one for Europe.

In February, the disaffected imperial generals were actually
preparing to strike a blow. Though they were apparently
unable to agree as to their ultimate objective, the name of
Napoleon was to be used as a rallying cry, and troops of the
16th Military District under Drouet d'Erlon whose headquarters were at Lille, together with those led by the Lalle-
mand brothers, were to march on Paris and seize the Tuileries.
News of their activities reached the ears of the government,
however, and Marshal Mortier was sent to Lille. The chief
conspirators thereupon lost their nerve and fled, only to be
captured a few days later. But in the midst of this excitement
came far more sensational news : Napoleon had escaped from
Elba and had landed on the Riviera coast at Fréjus.

CHAPTER II

THE HUNDRED DAYS

EVENTS now moved swiftly, from Napoleon's entry into Lyons to the defection of Ney with his army corps, as well as that of other regular troops. This grave news reached Paris on the 17th March and seems to have decided Louis XVIII, though he did not immediately reveal his intentions, to withdraw from Paris and go to Lille.

On the following evening, on returning from the palace, Richelieu observed to Rochechouart : " All this is going to end badly ; they have lost their heads at the Tuileries. I do not blame them ; events are moving so quickly, defections are increasing at such a rate, that it is impossible to do anything about it. I think, although neither the King nor his ministers have breathed a word to me, that they are going to retreat before the flood. Perhaps they will go to Lille, to await there the decision of the allied sovereigns still gathered in congress at Vienna. I cannot in decency abandon the King ; although he has told me nothing, I will stay with him to the end. Stempowski is going off now, with my valet, my carriage and my belongings ; they will await me at Frankfort. Lend me one of your three horses. I have managed to raise 10,000 francs in gold ; if you have any money, realise it and make your preparations. We may have to go at a few hours' notice." On this same day Chateaubriand also called at the Tuileries in the hope of obtaining some information about the King's movements, and complained of the unnecessary amount of mystery which was being made. Richelieu warned him : " Take care, they are deceiving us. For my part, I shall stand guard in the Champs Élysées, for I don't fancy receiving Buonaparte alone in the Tuileries."

On the next evening, Richelieu returned from the Tuileries at nine p.m. and said to Rochechouart : " Let us to horse and away ; there is not a moment to lose. I have talked for half an hour to the King, who did not say a word of his plans, but the Prince de Poix, Captain of the Bodyguard, whispered in my ear : ' We are off in an hour ; the relays are ready, we are going to Lille. Come and join us.' " The duke made ready and set off in such haste that he put on his belt inside out ; the gold pieces which he had stowed in it fell out into his boots and were only recovered from the bottom of them when he reached Beauvais.

But when Louis XVIII arrived at Lille, he found the attitude of the garrison so hostile that he decided to move on without delay, and the next day he crossed the frontier into Belgium. The Comte d'Artois and his younger son the Duc de Berry were following on his heels with the troops of the Royal Household, but when they got as far as Bethune they heard that Lille had raised the tricolour on the very day after the King's departure. The princes decided without more ado to follow the King out of the country. Artois thereupon disbanded the 3000 troops of the Royal Household, and crossed into Belgium with only 300 of the best mounted guards and musketeers. Richelieu, who had ridden the 180 miles to Ypres in five and a half days (" on the same horse, in the same shirt, which had scarcely dried on the journey," as he wrote to Langeron), was utterly disgusted at the pusillanimity of the princes. He overtook them at Ghent, where they had established themselves, and on coming from their presence was heard to express his opinion of them with unprintable vigour. Declaring that he wished to have no more to do with such people but would return to Russia, he went on to Brussels where Wellington and the British Guards had already arrived, and from there took the road to Vienna, whence the Tsar had not yet departed. He was slightly delayed at Liège through the officiousness of a Prussian officer who did not know him and who, after detaining him for thirty-six hours, had him escorted to Aix-la-Chapelle, a town which Richelieu was to

revisit three years later under very different circumstances.
From there, however, he continued on his way without further
mishap and duly reached Vienna in spite of the congestion on
the roads, which were heavily encumbered with troops on the
march once more towards the frontiers of France. On his
arrival in Vienna, Richelieu asked for permission to accom-
pany the Tsar on the forthcoming campaign and to remain at
his side, and this request having been granted, the duke set off
for Frankfort to collect his equipment, including his carriage.
Yet obviously the passage of eventful years had done nothing
to diminish the charms of Vienna, and though immediate
circumstances forbade the duke to prolong his stay there, it
was clearly as great a wrench as in days of old for him to have
to depart from the city. " I am sure that I do not need all
this great activity and occupation to be happy," he writes, " I
could lead a very pleasant life in Vienna with very little money.
I am fortunate never to be bored ; everything catches my
attention and amuses me. With this disposition, enough to
live on and a few friends, one could very well finish one's life
peaceably." It is not, he hastens to add, that he has any idea
of leaving Russia, or his post there, so long as he can do any
good in it and that any hope remains of his establishing his
name in a lasting fashion by the civilisation of that beautiful
countryside. But if coming events were going to render all
that impossible, then he would retire to Vienna, not without
some regrets, but in the certainty that there at least he would
not be unhappy.

On his way to Frankfort, all the countryside through which
he passed was like an armed camp ; drums were to be heard
everywhere and uniforms of all types to be seen. Once more
the Landwehr and Landsturm were being mobilised. The
allied sovereigns and their staffs had established their headquarters at Heidelberg, the Tsar having left Vienna on the
26th May. On his way to Heidelberg, he had paused at
Heilbronn, where he had his first meeting with Mme de
Krudener, the rather dubious religious mystic described by
the sceptical Castlereagh as " a high flyer in religion," but

who for a short time was to have a strong influence on the impressionable Alexander. In Heidelberg, the Tsar occupied a fine house outside the town, with delightful views of the river and of the mountainside covered with vines almost to its summit. Here in due course Richelieu presented himself to Alexander, who received him with his usual friendliness.

Soon after his arrival, a messenger arrived from Ghent, where Louis XVIII had established himself and his Court, bringing Richelieu documents nominating the duke as a Special Commissioner to be attached to the Tsar and the Russian forces, with the function of supervising the provinces occupied by the allied armies and the provisioning arrangements for those armies. Similar Commissioners it appeared were to be sent to the Austrian, Prussian and English armies. Richelieu felt no little embarrassment at the delicate position into which he found himself thrust. Obviously any such arrangement could only be implemented with the Tsar's approval; he therefore hastened to Alexander and placed the matter before him. The Tsar's reception of the proposal was chilly. It was, he said, impracticable from many points of view, not the least of which would be the unseemliness of anyone attached to his staff being charged with functions which might result in collisions with some of the allied generals. Furthermore, he asserted that the subject had actually been discussed at Vienna since his departure and that it had been rejected by the ministers of the allied Powers, as likely to do more harm than good. Richelieu was horrified to think that such proposals could have emanated from Ghent without any of the sovereigns concerned having been consulted.

He could not refrain from speaking to the Tsar on this occasion, too, about the attitude of the German Press, which even at that stage was breathing threats about the future dismemberment of France. In particular, he drew the Tsar's attention to an utterance of the *Berliner Zeitung* of the 20th May, in which, referring to Louis XVIII's statement that the Allies had undertaken to respect the integrity of French territory, the Prussian journal asserted that no such pledge had ever been given, that, on the contrary, the nations were relying on the wisdom of their princes to ensure the future peace of Europe by stronger guarantees than would be afforded by the mere restoration of the King. Alexander assured Richelieu that there could be no dismemberment of France, such an occurrence was unthinkable ; he had already told Richelieu at Vienna that not so much as a village would be taken. Richelieu replied that if such was the agreed intention of the Allies, the sooner they proclaimed it the better, as nothing would be more calculated to disarm French resistance. This was a point which the duke also stressed strongly to the Austrian Prince Schwarzenberg, in order, as he said, " to separate the allied cause from that of the usurper." Schwarzenberg, who was an old friend of Vienna days, was very amicable but said that nothing could be done without orders from Metternich, who professed to be too busy at that time to attend to such matters while the Emperor Francis was away with the army.

Although nearly a million men were being assembled to deal with the renewed menace of Napoleon, the great force would not be ready to move until the Russian troops had all arrived, in particular the Russian Imperial Guard for which their Emperor was waiting. Richelieu, with his restless energy, soon began to chafe at the prospect of having to spend two or three weeks waiting at headquarters, a penance which only the desire to be of some use to the King and to France would, he felt, enable him to support ; he would a thousand times rather have had even the smallest command. He therefore asked the Tsar for permission to return to Frankfort until all was ready. While waiting there, he employed some of his spare time in writing letters to Ghent, in an attempt to present the truth of the situation—if slightly watered down—to certain members of Louis XVIII's entourage, such as Blacas, whose presence had done so much to discredit the King's government. Though Richelieu considered that much of the public animus against Blacas was unfounded, there was no doubt of its existence and of the damage that Blacas was still doing to the royal cause by his

continued presence at the King's side. Richelieu saw Talleyrand as the one man suitable to lead the government of
France, since Talleyrand was in his own person a guarantee
to all those who had taken any part in the Revolution, and
he had a far better understanding of the new France than any
of the men who at that time surrounded the King. Talleyrand
himself arrived at Frankfort on the 15th June, and he and the
duke had a long conversation together. Richelieu was struck
with Talleyrand's lucid thinking and with the high quality of
his brain, only lamenting that such undoubted talent had not
always been applied in the right direction. Both Richelieu
and Talleyrand agreed that if the crown of France were to be
saved for Louis XVIII, not only Blacas but the princes must
be removed from the royal Council.

On the 20th June, Richelieu returned to Heidelberg, where
news of the first encounters in the Low Countries had just
begun to arrive and further details were being awaited with
the anxious impatience that can be imagined. The results of
Blücher's first meeting with Napoleon were anything but
encouraging, and all the following day, the 21st June, passed
without further news, so that at ten o'clock in the evening
Richelieu retired to bed. But he had scarcely done so when
throughout the town all the church bells began to ring,
salvoes of artillery thundered forth and wild cheering broke
out in the streets. Richelieu sat up listening for a moment,
then he could contain his impatient curiosity no longer and
leaping out of bed hurried in search of information. The
news of Waterloo had reached the town.

Richelieu, with a soldier's admiration for a battle well
fought, pays unstinted tribute to Wellington in his journal of
the Hundred Days : " Honour and eternal glory to Lord
Wellington and to his brave army ; " he writes, " it only
remained for him to beat Napoleon in pitched battle, and he
has seized the first opportunity of doing so. With 50,000 men
of different nations, more than half of whom had never been
under fire before, he sustained alone on the 18th the entire
effort of the very much stronger French army."

But when the first wave of thankful relief at the victory bringing the overthrow of the " Usurper " had spent itself, there remained inescapably the rocky question of what would now happen to France and to the Bourbons. As Wellington continued his march towards the French frontier and made plain his desire that the King should lose no time in returning, Richelieu began to writhe at the thought of a King of France re-entering his country at the heels of an English general and his army. Richelieu himself was entering France through Alsace with the Russians, who had crossed the Rhine at Speyer. On their way towards Nancy, they turned slightly south to Hagenau, where they encountered the deputation of left-wing leaders headed by Lafayette, Sébastiani and Voyer d'Argenson, who had come from Paris to negotiate. The principal aim of the deputation, it seemed, was to avert the succession of the Bourbons to the throne, though they were willing to have back Louis XVIII alone. These proposals seemed to Richelieu to be in tune with the feeling that he himself had detected during his recent stay in Paris ; but what was to be done with the princes remained a problem not easy to solve. In any case, however, the deputation received no definite answer since they were informed that nothing could be decided without first consulting England.

Meanwhile, on the 22nd June, the King and his Court, at Wellington's suggestion, made a move from Ghent to Mons on their road back to France, and here at last Louis XVIII was persuaded to part with Blacas, who, realising that he must go, obligingly saved everyone a great deal of trouble by tendering his resignation. On the 8th July, the King re-entered Paris, to be followed two days later by the three sovereigns of Russia, Austria and Prussia, who entered together. The same day, Léon de Rochechouart, who had also returned, was astounded to see in the list of new ministers published by the official government organ *Le Moniteur* the appointment of Richelieu to be Minister of the Royal Household, an office left vacant by the resignation of Blacas. Rochechouart expressed his stupefaction to Marshal Gouvion St. Cyr,

LOUIS XVIII.

saying he felt quite sure that Richelieu would not accept, not only because he was still in the service of the Tsar, but also because it was certain that nothing would induce the duke to serve in a government with Fouché. St. Cyr seems to have been equally shaken; no word, he said, had been mentioned about such a thing in the Council, but he would certainly bring it up that evening. Three days later, on the 13th July, Richelieu himself arrived in Paris, beside himself with vexation, and despite the Tsar's attempts to calm him, went the same evening to see the King, to whom he explained fully and frankly his reasons for feeling himself unable to accept the post. The King, while accepting Richelieu's refusal of the appointment in the royal household, still expressed the hope of having the duke in his Council. A few days later, on the 20th July, Richelieu wrote to Talleyrand, whom he justly suspected of being the real author of the arrangement, and set forth in detail his reasons for refusing. He had been absent from France, he said, for twenty-four years, making only two short re-appearances during that time. He was as much out of touch with people as with things and knew nothing about the administration of the government. Nobody, he emphasised, was less suited than himself to occupy any place in the ministry; if he did accept a post, it was certain that he would not hold it for more than six weeks. He was sorry if his refusal had made an unfortunate impression, but he felt that he was scarcely to blame for that, since the nomination had been made without consulting him while he had been still at Nancy. (But to make arrangements, even ministerial appointments, without consulting the people chiefly concerned was to be by no means a rare occurrence in the government of Restoration France.) In any case, Richelieu concluded, he had been in the Russian service for twenty-four years and for the last twelve of them had been occupied with a work he had very much at heart; he could not dream of abandoning it now. When Talleyrand replied, continuing to press the matter by demolishing one by one the defensive barriers Richelieu had raised, the duke in a second

letter written in August based his refusal on his obligations to
the Tsar, to whom, he said, he still had to give a proper
account of his administration in Russia, and this he could only
do when the Emperor had returned home. But to Langeron,
he unburdened his feelings more freely : " I am coming back
to Odessa," he wrote in early August, " I shall be there in
the course of November. That is what I have decided to do
after having seen this country, the difficulty of doing any
good, the little probability there is of having any success at
it, and the certainty of being in the process the most miserable
of men. If I could have been really useful to France, I would
have made the sacrifice, but as I am quite sure I can not, I
think I may be permitted to depart. . . . In this short reign
of three months there has been an appreciable change, and
very much for the worse. All the principles of Jacobinism,
suppressed for ten years, have reappeared. . . . God knows
what will become of this unfortunate country." People, he
said, were pinning their hopes on the new Chamber which
was about to assemble, but Richelieu felt that he could have
little faith in any system of representative government or
legislative assemblies for France, in view of the deplorable
lack of public spirit. In its place there was nothing to be
found but egotism and the love of money ; " I could tell you
of cases of venality which are enough to make you shiver."

But alas for Richelieu's hopes of escape and return to
Russia ; the net was about to descend upon him and entangle
him inexorably in its meshes. For the Chamber which was
the outcome of the August elections was the famous *Chambre
introuvable*, thus christened by the King himself because it
was so predominantly (and intolerantly) Royalist that its
like, he said, could not have been found. This composition
of the new Chamber had been deliberately fostered by the
revival of a practice allowed during the Empire of authorising
the Prefects of departments to add ten members to each
of the *collèges d'arrondissement* whose function it was to select
candidates for final election by the departmental colleges, each
of the latter being augmented similarly by twenty members.

Though in theory these additional members were supposed to be nominated for outstanding public service, their real qualification in the eyes of the Prefects was the extent to which they could be relied upon to vote Royalist. This manœuvre succeeded beyond all expectations : not only did the new Chamber have an overwhelming Royalist majority of the most extreme type, but since the minimum age of deputies had been reduced from forty to twenty-five, it contained a large proportion of fanatical young hot-heads.

With a Chamber of such ferociously Royalist hue, it was not surprising that the cabinet, composed almost entirely of moderates who had served Napoleon, and led by Talleyrand, should have become a primary target for their hostility. Fouché, the ex-regicide, was the chief object of their detestation. Yet it had been precisely the most extreme Royalists who were chiefly responsible for forcing Fouché on Louis XVIII in the ministry of the First Restoration, since in the words of Chateaubriand, without Fouché " there was neither safety for the King nor hope for France." Now, however, Fouché had become not only an object of loathing to the Royalist majority in the Chamber, but an embarrassing liability to his colleagues, and it was clear that he would have to be thrown overboard from the ministerial barque. But even without Fouché, the days of Talleyrand's cabinet were numbered. In the Chamber, he was faced by a bitterly hostile majority which he had tried to counterbalance by the wholesale creation of peers in the Upper House. Vitrolles, who was secretary to the Council in Talleyrand's cabinet, gives an astonishing account in his memoirs of the occasion when, on arriving one day for a Council meeting, he found Pasquier, busily writing, in occupation of his seat, while Talleyrand was standing at his side. Vitrolles enquired what they were doing ; Talleyrand replied placidly that they were making peers. So indeed they were, by the simple expedient of jotting down any likely names of friends or relations that occurred to them, each minister as he arrived adding his own selection. Yet it soon became clear that even these dubious

T.S.—9

measures would not save the life of the cabinet. However, knowing that the peace terms were bound to be very hard, Talleyrand was not unwilling to retire at this moment. Such retirement, he felt certain, could only be a temporary one. As he informed his colleagues, their successors would be left to reap the harvest of ill-will that would be sure to descend on the unfortunate ministers who had to carry through the treaty, and under such circumstances, declared Talleyrand confidently, the new cabinet would not last three months. There would then be only one solution remaining : " recourse to well-tried talent and experience." In other words, even those who were now most hostile would find themselves obliged to beg for Talleyrand's return to office. He therefore had no hesitation in adopting an attitude of defiance to the proposed peace terms, and the cabinet duly tendered their resignation ; which was accepted by the King with an alacrity which Talleyrand found slightly disconcerting.

But Louis XVIII was only too glad to have the problem solve itself so conveniently, and immediately after having received Talleyrand's resignation, he lost no time in sending for Richelieu. Then began the pleading and negotiation which was to continue for several days, as the unwilling victim struggled desperately against the meshes of the descending net. To the King's entreaties were added the almost frantic supplications of the Ultra-Royalists, the followers of the King's brother, the Comte d'Artois, now known as " Monsieur." Looking upon Richelieu as one of themselves, they no doubt felt assured that here was one who would do their will. Importuned unceasingly by two of the leading Ultras, Jules de Polignac and Mathieu de Montmorency, Richelieu told them with his usual forthright bluntness that they were making a mistake. " You don't know me. I shall not govern at all along the lines you hope, and you will regret your importunity." But Montmorency now fell on his knees before Richelieu and with clasped hands begged the duke to sacrifice his own inclinations and his peace of mind to save his country and his King. " Supposing you were on a battlefield," said Montmorency, "would you hesitate, if necessary, to order a charge and to put yourself at the head of the squadrons, even if to do so meant death ? Here the dangers are less ; a victory would be decisive for our country, without costing anybody's life." The Tsar then arrived on the scene and carried the duke off in his carriage for further persuasion. If Richelieu would become the King's minister as President of the Council, Alexander promised to be a friend both of the King and of France. He would do all in his power, he said, to save them both, to tone down the demands of the Allies and bring back to France her rightful place in the European concert of nations. He concluded his arguments by saying : " Intriguers of the worst kind have nearly brought about a break between the King and myself, by unjustifiable manœuvres harmful to the true interests of France. I can have no confidence in them, you alone can make me forget this act of ingratitude. I release you from all your engagements towards me, on condition that you serve your King as you have served me. You will be the link of a sincere alliance between the two countries ; I demand it in name of the welfare of France."

There was no resisting such arguments as these, and thus in spite of all his previous declarations, did inescapable fate descend upon the poor duke. At the very moment when he had thought to make his escape from a thoroughly uncongenial environment, he found himself trapped, torn away from the constructive task to which he had given his whole heart and energy, to be saddled in its place with one for which he felt himself to be the least suited of any man on earth. He had eluded the King's efforts to draw him back into the royal household only to find himself entangled in an even more repugnant undertaking. On the 21st September he wrote to the Abbé Nicolle : " The die is cast, M. l'abbé. I have yielded to the orders of the King, to the appeals of the Emperor and to the voice of the public which, I know not why, has called me to the ministry at this most frightful moment. . . . It would have been cowardly to abandon this unfortunate King in the horrible position he is in. The Emperor has been admirable to me on this occasion. He is allowing me to keep the 1600 ducats pension that I get and to apply it to the upkeep of the educational establishment [the Lycée] in Odessa. I advise you not to return to France : we are on top of a volcano. Farewell, M. l'abbé, pray to the good God for me ; I have never needed His aid so much. Poor France ! Poor Odessa ! Poor Crimea ! "

CHAPTER III

THE POLITICAL JUNGLE

SINCE Richelieu was now to hold the portfolio of Foreign Affairs as well as being President of the Council, he took up residence in the Hôtel Gallifet which, standing on the corner of the Rue du Bac and the Rue de Grenelle, was being used as the Ministry of Foreign Affairs. He was allowed 25,000 francs to get himself settled into the house and buy the necessary silver, glass, china and other equipment, and he entrusted the management of his household, as at Odessa, to Léon de Rochechouart. The latter was installed on the second floor of the house, and soon organised round himself the lively social life that was indispensable to him. But he dined every evening with the duke, " taking the place at his table of the mistress of the house."

From Mme de Montcalm's comments in her journal at this time, it seems that Richelieu's two sisters had rather expected that he might invite Mme de Jumilhac, the younger and more active of the two, to act as his hostess. Mme de Boigne says of her that " her mordant wit, imperturbable gaiety and a wholly natural animation made her the favourite of the most fashionable members of the best society," though she was, like her sister and sister-in-law, a hunchback and one who " paraded her appalling figure without the smallest embarrassment at every social gathering." But apart from Mme de Jumilhac's deformity, it may well have been precisely on account of her " mordant wit " that Richelieu did not invite her to do the honours of his house. Mme de Montcalm seems to have thought that because he had for so many years led a life of austere simplicity in a predominantly male environment, Richelieu had become little accustomed to feminine society. Yet as we have seen, the duke on occasion could enjoy social

life as much as anyone.   But he had at all times a horror of
tittle-tattle and intrigue, and as is shown by a letter he wrote
to Langeron at this time he was greatly shocked at the attitude
being taken in political life by the women of the aristocracy,
who far from exerting their influence towards healing the
wounds of the past, were infinitely more embittered reaction-
aries than the men, constantly urging them on to the most
extravagant degrees of Ultra-Royalism.   As long as Richelieu
was a minister, he could not be persuaded to invite any women
to social gatherings under his own roof, and in order that he
might not be accused of being under feminine influence, he
particularly asked both his sisters not to forward any petitions
to him.   This request, says Mme de Montcalm, put them in a
very embarrassing position, since every day they were being
inundated with applications for favours.   The position both of
Richelieu himself and of his two sisters was in fact an extremely
difficult one.   Their social connections were naturally with the
aristocracy, among whom the most rabid Ultra-Royalists
abounded, and as it presently became clear that the duke was
not going to associate himself with a policy of embittered
reaction, not only he but his two sisters were made to suffer
the increasing animosity of many who would normally have
been found among their circle of friends.

Richelieu's elder sister, Armandine, Marquise de Montcalm, with whom it became his custom to spend most of his
evenings, devoted herself to providing her brother with a congenial background where he might be able to forget some of
the vexations of his daily life as a minister.   In her *salon*,
gathered round the couch on which she lay, with her deformity
almost entirely concealed by a discreet arrangement of wraps,
would be found notables of the diplomatic world, chief among
them Pozzo di Borgo, the Tsar's minster in Paris, and a
certain number of Royalists.   These latter were mostly, and in
greater proportion as time went on, of the more moderate
type, such as Lainé, Pasquier and Cardinal de Bausset.   Yet so
ardent an Ultra as Hyde de Neuville was to remain her devoted
friend through all the storms of political life.   Chateaubriand

THE MARQUISE DE MONTCALM
(From a lithograph by Lemercier)

also frequented her *salon* so long as he thought Mme de Montcalm's supposed influence with her brother might be useful, particularly in restoring him to the favour of the King whom he had deliberately flouted with the publication of his *Monarchie selon la Charte*, a scarcely veiled attack on the royal favourite, Decazes. Mme de Boigne, while admitting that Richelieu's sister had a handsome face and a cultivated mind, asserts that she was exacting and anxious for admiration. Yet others, both men and women, who knew Mme de Montcalm are agreed that she possessed great charm, and could be both gay and witty. If there were times when she was less gay and tended, like her brother, to look on the world through dark spectacles, that is hardly surprising, for life had not treated her kindly. Her children had all died either at or soon after birth, she and her husband had since separated, and now suffering much from ill-health, she was often in pain. But having lived through so much of the political turmoil to which Richelieu had returned as a stranger, she could not help feeling that he took an unduly pessimistic view of conditions in France. It seemed to her that he paid too much attention to the gossip of the *salons*; clouds on the horizon were apt to assume for him the proportions of tempests, while men's failings became incurable vices. All this was destroying his peace and happiness. What he needed was to be calmed and softened.

Yet it was certainly not easy to preserve one's calm amongst the Kilkenny cats of the political jungle. The deep imprint left on French political life by the storms of the preceding quarter century had produced a number of constantly shifting groups, each deeply suspicious of one another. Each group had its own rallying-point outside the Chamber in various *salons* where deputies of the same shade of opinion could meet, and in 1818, Count Molé, who had served in the Napoleonic administration, was to lament to Mme de Rémusat that he had never known a time when political opinions were so diverse. No two people, he said, thought the same, and the divergence of their views became apparent in the first few words of any discussion.

The Royalists were themselves divided between the most extreme section, known as the Ultras, gathered round Monsieur, the King's brother, and the moderate constitutionalists who struggled to hold a balance between the rabid Ultras on the extreme fringe of their own party and the heirs of the Revolution on the Left. The Ultras made no secret of their contempt for the new constitutional system of government embodied in the Charter, and Monsieur soon formed his own court of the most extreme Royalists. Many of these men had spent the years of the emigration either fighting in the Royalist armies or moving about Europe on secret missions. Unfortunately, the habits of these perilous years were not easily discarded and methods of underground intrigue often came more naturally to them than that of parliamentary opposition, in spite of the large Ultra majority in the Chamber. Monsieur's *gouvernement occulte* was thus to become a thorn in the side of every ministry that took office, not least that of Richelieu who was soon complaining that Monsieur was always the party leader, never the heir apparent to the crown of France. For the very Ultras who had been foremost in imploring Richelieu to take office were to become his most determined opponents from the moment they realised that the duke neither shared in, nor proposed to encourage, their rancorous spirit of revenge. Their attitude, intensified as a result of the Hundred Days, greatly horrified him and at the end of 1815 he wrote to the Ultra leader, Villèle : " Truly, you and your friends are mad. I have been ruined by the Republic ; returning to France after a long exile, I find my château demolished, my town house sold, my pictures and my libraries in the museums and other public buildings ; yet I cannot understand how the feeling of sorrow which must be felt by the victims of such misfortunes can lead to those feelings of vengeance which could bring a return of the same evils."

In view of these sentiments, frequently expressed, Richelieu caused a certain amount of surprise in moderate circles by his outspoken condemnation of Marshal Ney ; but as he explained in a letter which he wrote to the Tsar on the 23rd

November, he had taken this stand firstly because he felt that justice must take its course (there could be no denying the heinous military aspect of the Marshal's offence), but even more because, having thus given satisfaction to " the party " who were clamouring for chastisements, he hoped that he would then be able to call a halt to further measures and persuade the King to grant a general amnesty. If by any chance the Chamber were to be so carried away by blind passion as to reject such a measure, then, he declared to the Tsar, he would soon be taking the road back to Russia, " for no human power can make me adopt a system of persecution and vengeance which would cause rivers of blood to flow and bring ruin to France and to the royal family." Richelieu was as good as his word : the very day after Ney's execution, he brought forward a law of amnesty, thinking that now an example had been made, the Chamber would be prepared for some show of clemency. But he had even then underestimated the violence of Ultra passions, and it soon became clear that the very fate of the ministry was linked with the passing of the law. Fortunately the King, with his sound good sense, gave Richelieu strong support, and the law was eventually carried in January. But the princes, true to form, were ranged in the strongest opposition ; which, as Richelieu reported unhappily to the Tsar, did not cease to " render my position difficult, and above all, horribly disagreeable." To Villèle he remarked with his usual forthright candour that the princes seemed to have forgotten that they had only returned to France in the baggage wagons of the foreign armies—a blunt statement of fact which Villèle, the good Ultra, found " quite inconceivable in the mouth of one of the King's ministers."

The large number of groups which constituted the Left also contained many varying shades of opinion. The moderates who for the first few years of the Restoration formed the left half of a Centre party, were alone entitled to the name of " Liberals " in anything approaching the modern sense ; for at this time the name was used indiscriminately, like the sinister word " Jacobin," as a comprehensive label for the entire political jungle which made up the various groups of the Left. The extreme section of the party was at first divided into three distinct groups of Republicans, Bonapartists and Orleanists ; but under the stress of the Hundred Days and the embittered Royalist reaction which followed, the first two combined. The Orleanist section of the Left was supported by bankers and rich industrials whose primary interest was naturally in the establishment of orderly and stable govern-ment under which alone their commerce and industry could flourish.

For the first few years of the Restoration, yet another party, the so-called Doctrinaires, followed a middle path between the moderates of Right and Left. They looked upon the Restoration as a bridge between the old France and the new, and the Charter as the chief plank in that bridge. The group included some really able men such as Royer-Collard, Guizot, Barante and Camille Jordon, the latter a friend of Fox and Lord Holland and a fervent admirer of the English con-stitution. Unfortunately however, the Doctrinaires, sublimely convinced of the infallible correctness of their own views and principles, in no way regarded their cause as identical with that of the government, but as Guizot himself admits, would criticise its policy even while defending it—if they were not attacking it outright. The more vital and delicate the question at issue, the greater became the peril of their dissidence, and to Richelieu their carping criticism was both irritating and frustrating.

Since, after his long absence from France, Richelieu had returned as a complete stranger to the domestic political scene, he found himself in a very difficult position when called upon so unexpectedly to form a cabinet. When he had revisited France in 1802, trying to recover some of his property, he had conducted litigation over the duchy of Fronsac through a lawyer of the name of Decazes. The son of this man had also followed a legal career and had done so well for himself that during the time of the Empire he became secretary to the household of Napoleon's mother. He did not, however,

return to the imperial cause during the Hundred Days, and at
the Second Restoration he was made Prefect of Police through
the influence of Baron Louis, who had formed a good opinion
of him. Since the Minister of Police was the detested Fouché
who had been forced upon Louis XVIII, the King formed the
habit of using the young Prefect as a means of keeping himself
acquainted with the political situation at home, upon which it
was at that time the business of the police to report. (His
Majesty also derived the keenest enjoyment from hearing about
the domestic scandals of his subjects, as revealed from the
police censorship of their correspondence.) Decazes was a
young man of good looks and engaging manners, and it was
not long before he had taken the place of the lost Blacas in the
royal affections. He had therefore been the chief intermediary during the days of negotiations to persuade Richelieu
to take office, and when the duke finally yielded he insisted
that Decazes should receive the portfolio of Police in his
cabinet. Unfortunately, in order to placate Monsieur, it was
also thought desirable to bestow the portfolios of the Interior,
War and Marine respectively, on the three Ultras, Vaublanc,
Feltre and Dubouchage. This was not a happy arrangement,
since within a few weeks the cabinet became split into two
factions: the three Ultras on the one side, against the moderates
led by Richelieu and supported by Decazes, Corvetto and
Barbé-Marbois. Corvetto, who had been a Councillor of
State during the Empire, was an able financier whose services
were to be invaluable in the difficult tasks that lay immediately
ahead ; but none of the three Ultras could have been described
as an asset to the cabinet. Vaublanc was a particularly bad
bargain who, as the duke said of him in a moment of special
exasperation, had only accepted office " in order to give proof
of the most complete ineffectiveness and intrepid vanity."

It was not going to be easy to govern France with a cabinet
so soon divided in itself, however, and it was made infinitely
more difficult by the ministers' inexperience of the machinery
of constitutional and cabinet government. This was probably
the real root of much of the irresolution and vacillation of

which Richelieu was accused; Marmont very aptly compared
him to a man given the task of finding his way in the dark
about a building with whose layout he is imperfectly
acquainted. Count Molé, who had had long experience of
administration under Napoleon, gives a strange picture of the
meetings of Richelieu's cabinet, which met three times a week.
All members, he says, would arrive at the appointed time
except Decazes, who was not infrequently one or even two
hours late. They would wait for him during half or three-
quarters of an hour, then Richelieu, losing patience, would turn
his chair abruptly towards the table and open the meeting.
When Decazes eventually appeared, he would pass to Richelieu
the portfolio of police reports he had just been showing to the
King, and then sitting down without a word of apology for his
delay, he would begin to deal with his correspondence without
paying the least attention to what was being discussed round
him. Richelieu would then occupy himself with reading
the police reports just handed to him, while Pasquier warmed
himself by the fire, Gouvion St. Cyr slept in a chair and Molé
walked up and down. Any minister who had some matter to
discuss and needed to have a cabinet decision upon it was thus
obliged first to beg for the attention of Richelieu and Decazes.
Molé adds that when he found this to be the usual procedure
at cabinet meetings, he followed the example of his colleagues,
only listening when he was personally concerned in the discussions and spending most of the time pacing up and down.
He and Corvetto—who having like himself served under
Napoleon, had thus as he says " known a different method of
conducting business "—could scarcely conceal their irritation
and would express their feelings by the exchange of significant
glances. When Lainé had become Minister of the Interior, he
wrote to Cuvier that the King wished him to support a law
which was to be presented in the Chamber on the following
day; but he omitted to mention what the law was that Cuvier
was to be required to support at such short notice. Fortunately Cuvier seems to have been blessed with a sense of humour
and saw the funny side of the situation. But the Comte de

Serre took a different view when a few days later Corvetto, as
Minister of Finance, asked him to undertake the defence of the
budget, without troubling to ask his consent and without even
acquainting him with the basic details of the budget he was to
support.

Even the King, who prided himself on his knowledge of
the workings of constitutional government in England, made
his own contribution to the unorthodox methods practised by
his ministers. Thus in 1817 he ensured the safe passage of
the electoral law through the Upper House by the simple
expedient of forbidding all members of his family and household to attend the debates upon it. In 1818, at the urgent
request of Decazes and in order to avert a possible government
defeat over St. Cyr's military law, he took out with him in his
carriage, despite torrential rain, three peers in attendance on
him whose votes, it was suspected, might otherwise tilt the
scales against the Ministry. On this occasion, however,
the peers proved to be as resourceful as their King : they
arranged to have carriages waiting for them in the palace
courtyard, and leaping into these immediately on their return
from the royal promenade, they were driven at top speed to
the Luxembourg, where they arrived just in time to record
their votes. Nevertheless, the law just scraped through the
Upper House, curiously enough by a majority of exactly three
votes—which, as Louis XVIII wrote subsequently to Decazes,
enabled " that pest Talleyrand " to go about declaring that its
survival was due solely to " the King's carriage."

But for good or ill, Richelieu was now committed to the
task of carrying the burden from which circumstances had
enabled the adroit Talleyrand to disengage himself. To
Richelieu had fallen the fearful responsibility of leading the
government of France at what he described as " this most
frightful moment," and the poor duke confided to Molé that
the day on which he finally took the decision to do so was the
unhappiest of his life.

CHAPTER IV

THE PEACE TREATY

RICHELIEU and his cabinet were now faced with the odious task of making the best terms possible with a ring of exasperated European nations whose attitude, after the fresh upheaval of the Hundred Days, had greatly hardened.

The German states, headed by Prussia, were particularly relentless. Providence, declared the Prussian Chancellor Hardenberg, had laid in the hands of other nations this opportunity of curbing France ; it must not be thrown away. France must be penned inside a frontier which her neighbours could defend against her, and must give up not only Alsace, but the fortresses of the Low Countries, the Meuse, the Moselle and the Sarre. Metternich also expressed the opinion that the permanent interest of Europe demanded that France's first-line fortresses must either be ceded to her neighbours or dismantled, while some in the second line must be demolished as well ; since even then France, with her remaining strong points and the passes of the Vosges, would have more than sufficient bulwarks to keep her on an equal footing with other first-class Powers. King William of the Netherlands, while in hearty agreement with his Allies on the question of Alsace, Lorraine and the frontier fortresses, was also turning an acquisitive eye on Flanders and Artois ; even then, he maintained, France would still remain the most powerful state in Europe.

But the Tsar, not unmindful of his pledge to Richelieu, opposed these drastic proposals. As early as July he had declared that he would withdraw both himself and his army if his Allies did not moderate their demands. He had shown Richelieu a map upon which had been traced the proposed amputations of French territory, signed by the representatives of the Powers concerned, and had declared to the duke : " There is only one signature lacking, and I swear to you that it will always be lacking." Since then, however, the Tsar had fallen under the influence of Mme de Krudener, and in his absorption with higher spheres and the project of a Holy Alliance, had for the time being lost touch with the more practical aspects of affairs. A good deal, therefore, would now depend on the attitude taken up by England.

The British cabinet felt strongly that France ought not to be let off too lightly this time. They considered that the frontier fortresses should remain in Allied hands, and that the whole French frontier ought to be occupied. The Prime Minister, Lord Liverpool, was even in favour of depriving France of the conquests of Louis XIV, so as to reduce her to a position in which a war of revenge would be impossible.

France was therefore in real danger of being partially dismembered by her irate neighbours. But fortunately for her at this critical moment the calm commonsense of Wellington reacted strongly against the idea of territorial, or even permanent fortress cessions. In his opinion, there should be no change in the first Treaty of Paris. The French nation, as a whole, had not really supported Napoleon on his return ; if they had done so, he declared, the allied armies could never have reached Paris in a fortnight. If territory were now to be taken from France, she would ultimately unite under an aggressive government whose aim would be to recover it. What was needed was a temporary occupation of certain regions. The British Foreign Secretary, Lord Castlereagh, strongly supported Wellington's idea of a temporary occupation, and he explained to Louis XVIII that the Allies, whose primary aim was security, were choosing temporary occupation as an alternative to permanent cessions of territory. For the King was protesting vigorously against the severity of the proposed peace terms, and on 23rd September he wrote personally to the Tsar that he would sooner abdicate than be the instrument of his people's ruin.

Louis XVIII's appeal seems to have roused Alexander from his celestial abstractions and to have reminded him of the promise of support he had given to Richelieu. While agreeing with Castlereagh's idea of certain frontier adjustments, he reiterated his intention of withdrawing his army if his Teutonic allies persisted in their territorial demands. As a result of the Tsar's attitude and the combined efforts of Wellington and Castlereagh, France was saved from the amputations of territory for which the German states had been clamouring. The fulfilment of Alexander's promise to Richelieu resulted in the preservation for France not only of all her frontier fortresses except Huningen, but of the provinces of Alsace and Lorraine, so retaining as part of her eastern frontier a considerable stretch of the Rhine. Thus, as it has been well said, Odessa paid in advance the ransoms of Strasbourg and Metz.

But there were grave financial as well as territorial issues to be considered in the treaty, and the basic clauses of these were laid down at the beginning of October. France undertook to pay a war indemnity, to maintain and pay the armies of occupation, and also to settle claims brought forward by the various allied governments on behalf of their respective nationals, the amount of these sums to be assessed by commissions representing each government. To these clauses, after what Richelieu described as " most painful discussions," he reluctantly agreed, since the Tsar's two lieutenants, Pozzo di Borgo and Capodistrias assured him that under the existing circumstances no better terms could be hoped for. But on the following day, he wrote to the Tsar that he had only signed the convention because " it was impossible to prolong any further the state of desolation in which France finds herself, and I have had to agree to everything in order to make an end of it." In the final form of the treaty, the war indemnity was cut down to 700 millions, while the period of military occupation was reduced from seven years to five, with the possibility of its termination in three years if the allied sovereigns thought fit. As soon as the general lines of the treaty had thus been laid down, the allied sovereigns departed from Paris. But negotiations over the working-out of the details continued all through the month into November, and Mme de Montcalm laments that during that time she scarcely set eyes on her brother for more than a quarter of an hour in the week.

On the 20th November, Richelieu attached his signature to the Second Treaty of Paris. " All is finished," he wrote afterwards, " more dead than alive, I have put my name to this fatal treaty. I had sworn not to do it and had said as much to the King, but the unhappy prince, dissolving in tears, begged me not to abandon him, and from that moment I did not hesitate." On the 25th, Richelieu had the painful duty of reading the treaty to the Chambers. It was received with gloomy resignation, but the speech with which the duke accompanied it showed a stern appreciation of realities. It was, he said, the result of circumstances unparalleled in history. They had all been witnesses of the explosion of universal wrath at the re-appearance of France's evil genius, when Europe thought to see herself once more subjugated by soldiers carried away by the same illusions and animated by the same enthusiasm as before. A common instinct of self-preservation had at once concentrated upon the one object all the fears, the hates, the interests of the terrified nations. Political rivalries were forgotten ; all the resources of the peoples were mobilised, their populations of all ages, all classes, had been driven by the same impulsion, and more than a million soldiers had hurled themselves upon the frontiers of France. The price which now had to be paid was a heavy one, but " Reflect, gentlemen, on the dire impression made upon an astonished and irritated Europe by the catastrophe of which France has just been the victim, and even more, upon the ease with which the seditious have carried all before them in their own country." The duke concluded : " We have had enough of ambition, of the fatal glory that is acquired by feats of arms and by the bloody trophies of their victories. There remains for us to achieve a greater glory; let us compel the nations, in spite of the evil done to them by the usurper, to regret what they are now doing to us; let us compel them to trust us, to know us well, to become reconciled with us sincerely and for ever." Richelieu himself received a memorable souvenir of his ordeal when the Tsar bestowed on him the map upon which had been traced the proposed dismemberment of France—a precious document still preserved in the Richelieu family archives.

Yet the task which lay in front of Richelieu and his ministry was still only beginning. They were now faced with the problem of putting France's financial house in order, to raise money both for the payment of the indemnity which alone could bring release from the foreign occupation and for the settlement of the liquidations. Although the final figure of the war indemnity had been reduced in the treaty, the total amount of liquidations still remained to be assessed, a procedure which was to be the source of several years' acrimonious discussion. Some of the claims, which in the first instance totalled some 1600 million francs, were even more fantastic in nature than in amount: the Duke of Anhalt-Bernburg, for instance, applied for money outstanding to his ancestors in respect of German troopers hired by Henri IV for the struggle against the Catholic League!

Richelieu began by appealing to the Ambassadors' Conference. When they replied in effect that the matter was outside their jurisdiction and had been provided for in the treaty, Richelieu pointed out that the enormous size of the sums demanded far exceeded anything foreseen in the Treaty of Paris. He declared that he could not possibly face the Chambers with a demand for forty or fifty millions of *rentes*; he was so certain that such a demand would be flatly rejected that he would rather resign than lay the country open to the disturbances which would inevitably follow such a request. He maintained that some modification of the convention was therefore essential if France was to be able to fulfil her engagements. At first, the allied governments showed little inclination to any revision of the agreement,

and even Wellington, for the time being, remained aloof.
Only Pozzo di Borgo, the Tsar's ambassador in Paris, ranged
himself on Richelieu's side ; but this was an embarrassment
rather than a help, since the one point on which the other
three ambassadors and Wellington were in the heartiest
agreement was in their intense dislike of Pozzo and of what
they regarded as his mischievous meddling.

As if France were not already struggling with enough
difficulties at this moment, the weather brought equally
serious and perhaps still more urgent ones. For, after a poor
harvest in 1815, the summer of 1816 turned out to be one
of the worst for years, with an almost incessant downpour of
heavy rain. Not only was the corn crop again very poor,
but the grape harvest was practically ruined. All this naturally resulted in great hardship, the chief feature of which was
an acute shortage and consequent rise in the price of bread.
Richelieu appealed urgently to Langeron, who had succeeded
him as Governor of Odessa, to speed up the transport of
grain, which was brought to France not only from the Black
Sea but also from the Baltic, Holland and even from the
United States. To the Abbé Nicolle, who was still in Odessa,
he wrote at this time that the nation was enduring these
hardships in stoical resignation, since " there is no energy
here for anything but hatred. This passion is still in all its
strength, as much alive as in 1792, and society is intolerable.
. . . Those who believe you can undo a twenty-five-year-old
revolution with two or three decrees are furious that we do
not lend ourselves to such a simple operation. They set me
up, thinking to make me the instrument of their extravagances,
and seeing now that I am not having any, and even that I
should like to save them in spite of themselves by following
a line of moderation and sense, they are raving against me.
. . . All this is no doubt a trifling matter ; but when this
hostility comes from men of the class with whom you are
destined to live, and when, moreover, the aberrations of this
class can have such serious consequences, one cannot help
deploring them." Richelieu again advised the Abbé Nicolle

not to return to France, since not only was the country a smouldering volcano, but he felt certain that when the King died there would be a terrible explosion. " A certain party," it appeared, was openly speculating about that event and making no secret of the opinion that it was too long in coming to pass. Meanwhile the unhappy King, pulled this way by his relatives, that way by his ministers, longed only for peace but found it nowhere ; all of which was doing no good to his already failing health. As for Richelieu himself he was, he declared, even more miserable than the King, since he felt that there was no one round him to whom he dared open his heart. His letters to the Marquis d'Osmond show also that he was much concerned about the safe custody of Napoleon, fearing that the prisoner was not being sufficiently well guarded, and that there might be a repetition of the escape from Elba ; or even that a change of government in England —whose domestic politics were watched by Richelieu with anxious concern—might result in the release of the captive. As the duke was to write in 1818 : " I cannot prevent myself from thinking continually of that rock and of the evils that negligence or treachery could allow to escape from it."

In view of the great distress reigning in France, Richelieu appealed to the Powers, asking for a three months' respite from payments. Russia, Austria and England agreed to accept 270 millions instead of 300 millions for the maintenance of their armies in 1817, and after much discussion Prussia was persuaded to do the same ; though the German states had not been backward in taking the fullest advantage of the opportunity of having their troops paid and maintained at the expense of France. Naturally, as Castlereagh observed dryly, so long as they could continue to do this while at the same time receiving English subsidies, they were in no hurry for a final settlement. Indeed, they had quite unnecessarily increased the size of their detachments, thus bringing the total number of allied troops in France up to 900,000 men. Moreover Prussia and Austria were still claiming 200 and 150 millions respectively for their liquidations. Richelieu wrote again to Osmond in London asking him to beg Castlereagh to continue to exert his wise influence, for which France had already so much reason to be grateful, in order that the European edifice reconstructed with such painful care should not again come toppling to the ground ; as it might well do under the weight of a burden which, declared the duke, it was quite beyond the power of France to support. If she were pushed to extremities, the whole nation would burst into flames and no one could tell how far the fire might then spread. Once again, too, Richelieu wished to draw attention to what his own position was likely to be if he had to face the Chambers with a demand for forty or fifty millions worth of *rentes* for the settlement of private individuals' debts—an aspect he felt certain that Castlereagh, with his long parliamentary experience, would appreciate. Richelieu concluded by saying that as Metternich, Capodistrias and Hardenberg were all to meet at Carlsbad in August, he would get Caraman to call there on the way to Vienna.

But when Caraman arrived in Carlsbad on the 17th August, he was informed that Hardenberg was ill and could not see him ; while Jordan, Hardenberg's right-hand man, was hostile, maintaining that the convention had been signed and ratified and could not therefore be tampered with. Richelieu now hoped that Metternich might be persuaded to use his influence with Hardenberg, but the cautious Austrian Chancellor would make no move without knowing the official opinion of Prussia ; for he could not afford to alienate those Germans who were clamouring for their money, since he needed their support for the re-establishment of Austrian leadership in Germany. He therefore soothed Caraman with fair words, while at the same time recommending the greatest discretion to Baron Vincent, the Austrian ambassador in Paris, telling him to request France to resume the suspended payments. But when Metternich had seen Jordan, he declared that Austria was " morally obliged to sustain the Prussian cause," and Vincent was therefore obliged to fall into line with Goltz, his Prussian colleague.

In this difficult situation, Richelieu once more turned for support to the Tsar, who sent a note to London suggesting that the services of Wellington should be enlisted. The British Government agreed that the problem should be referred to Wellington's arbitration. Richelieu maintained that France could not produce more than 200 millions, though Prussia was still standing out for 130 millions for herself alone. Wellington, with his practical commonsense, said that the Powers must first agree on possible reductions and then proceed to a last revision. All through January and February 1818, while Richelieu and Corvetto were preparing details of their side of the case, Wellington and the ambassadors worked on theirs. Richelieu wrote to Osmond that Wellington " seeks the truth in a spirit of justice and integrity which, in my view, does him the greatest honour. I do not know what will be the outcome of his arbitration, but what I do know is that he has given me an even higher idea of his noble character than I had before, and in truth that is saying not a little." The result finally achieved was a considerable reduction in the claims of the various nations. Austria was persuaded to accept twenty-five millions instead of the 200 she had been demanding ; Switzerland, who had claimed 100 millions, agreed to accept fifty ; while Saxony and Hanover agreed to three millions instead of fifteen. This brought the total amount from 773 millions to 216, which was at least within sight of the sum offered by Richelieu.

But just as a settlement seemed at last to be approaching, fresh difficulties arose over the French refusal to pay two years' interest on the reclamations ; an attitude which Wellington viewed with considerable irritation and disgust. " I think both the King and his Ministers have behaved shabbily in this concern," he wrote to Castlereagh, " the Ministers of the Allies have certainly come down as low as they can, or ought, and they all reckoned upon and have a right to the back interest. But the King and his Ministers take advantage of the general eagerness to obtain a settlement to refuse any reasonable accommodation upon the question."

In his letters to Osmond, however, Richelieu set forth his side of the case : that such a payment would mean finding another thirty million francs, or a further two million *rentes*. The sixteen millions of *rentes* for which in any case he would have to ask the Chambers would be more than enough, he declared, to produce the most violent outbursts at the tribune. These would have to be borne ; but if he were to ask for yet another two millions, the very existence of the King's government would be threatened. Such statements might sound far-fetched, yet it was perfectly true that in 1816 Richelieu's cabinet had been nearly brought down over the budget by the truculent *Chambre introuvable*. Richelieu had written to Osmond at the time that the budget was being used as a weapon for the overthrow of the ministry, which would surely fall, since all the powerful people were amongst its attackers, the most powerful one of all withholding his support. In the parliamentary session of 1818, too, the allocation of two million francs usually made in the budget for police intelligence services was made the occasion by the Ultras for yet another violent attack, this time on Decazes as Minister of Police. In the matter of the back interest, Richelieu did not deny that right was on the side of the Allies ; but since the affair was being dealt with by arbitration, he maintained that in view of the circumstances some latitude should be allowed. So strongly indeed did he feel on this point that he declared that if Wellington had not finally yielded, he would have referred the issue to the sovereigns when they met in congress.

Prussia and certain other German Powers continued for a further while to raise one objection after another to the final settlement proposed ; but they were at last silenced when Wellington and Pozzo di Borgo combined in threatening to exclude from the general liquidation those who persisted in making difficulties.

CHAPTER V

LIBERATION OF THE TERRITORY

THE problem of the liquidations, vast as it was, merely constituted one aspect of the tangled financial skein in which was bound up the most vital issue of all : the termination, within as short a period as possible, of the foreign occupation of French territory.

The figure finally agreed upon for the size of the occupying forces had been 150,000 men. But it soon became plain to Richelieu that however desirable it might be—and according to the Ultras it was vital for the safety of the monarchy—for an allied force to police the country until conditions had settled down, the maintenance of so large an army, added to the other crushing financial obligations, was throwing an intolerable strain on the shattered finances of France. Moreover, as Richelieu wrote to Langeron at Odessa, it was such a humiliating position to be in that one would have thought it would weigh on Frenchmen above everything else : " not at all ; they are occupied with their party quarrels, with ousting this one from his place to give it to that one ; they tear one another asunder, the violence of their passions is inextinguishable. They remind me of the Byzantine Greeks who cut one another's throats in their circuses for the sake of the green or blue colours of the charioteers while the Moslems were at their gates. The Paris *salons* are arenas where they are always ready to have one another's heads for the sake of a differing shade of opinion. Thus I never set foot in them. Anyway I should get a bad reception in many of them, for you must know that I am a kind of Jacobin because I do not share the exaggerations and follies of people who, although they have done nothing and seen nothing, think themselves called upon to rule nations." Mme de Montcalm tells how on one occasion when Richelieu was on his way to a reception given by one of the prominent English hostesses in Paris, his carriage was driven by mistake to the next house, where the Princesse de la Trémoille, " queen of the Ultras," happened also to be giving a grand supper. The duke, on entering the room and looking round for his hostess, suddenly realised into what a hornet's nest he had blundered. Without uttering a word, he turned rapidly on his heels and made his exit as fast as his legs could carry him !

Yet however much the Ultras might favour the continuance of the occupation, it appeared likely to defeat its own purpose by the inevitable friction arising, from a variety of causes both serious and trivial, between the occupying forces and the population of the country. Richelieu himself, at the beginning of the occupation, had had personal experience of what might have been an unpleasant incident when he happened to be on a visit to Courteilles and a detachment of Prussian troops arrived on the scene demanding provisions ; in default of which they threatened, in their inimitable way, to burn and pillage the château. Great was their surprise, however, when they were suddenly confronted with the imposing figure of the duke who, throwing open his coat so as to display the Russian decorations glittering on his chest, signed to the invaders by an imperious gesture to withdraw ; which they lost no time in doing, since strangely enough their commanding-officer turned out to be an old comrade-in-arms of the duke. On a later occasion, Richelieu had felt obliged to remonstrate with Wellington over the activities of a certain British colonel by the name of Woodford who, having bought the right of digging on the field of Agincourt, was proceeding (not very tactfully) to excavate the site where according to Froissart a number of French knights had been buried, and had already unearthed a collection of spurs, stirrup-irons and other fragments. " You have no idea what a noise this is making," said our French duke to his English counterpart ; " I must beg you to put a stop to it." So, as

Wellington said when speaking of the incident in later years,
" I gave Woodford a hint to dig no more."

As early as January 1816, Richelieu had in fact persuaded
Wellington to consent to the withdrawal of troops from Paris
itself, and Wellington had then set up his headquarters at
Cambrai.   Richelieu next began to press for a reduction in
the actual numbers of the occupying troops.   In July, after a
period of relative quiet, even Wellington did not seem
unfavourably disposed to the idea, writing to Richelieu that he
thought the British Government would probably be very
willing to meet his wishes if none of the other Powers objected.
But this prospect did not find favour at all in the sight of the
Ultras.   Their frame of mind was well epitomised by Mme de
Rémusat when, speaking of the Ultras in Toulouse, which
had always been a hot-bed of the most extreme royalism, she
wrote to her son Charles : " I can see certain people here
arriving at the necessity of a little Saint Bartholemew.   The
great phrase of the moment, ' They will kill us, if we do not
kill them,' is at the bottom of all that."   This obsessing fear,
which had found expression in the White Terror of 1815 and
in the bloodthirsty speeches with which the truculent Ultra,
La Bourdonnaie, sought to justify it in the Chamber, made
the Ultras look upon Richelieu's efforts to reduce the numbers
of the allied forces in France as an invitation to disaster.
Monsieur, however, was at the same time entirely convinced
that the duke's ministry was tottering and that only a final
push was required ; a push which would be all the stronger
if support could be enlisted across the Channel.   At the very
time, therefore, when Wellington was writing favourably to
Richelieu about a possible reduction in the allied forces,
Monsieur was sending an emissary, Vicomte de Bruges, over
to England to spread the most depressing reports about the
condition of France.   He was to announce that only the
prompt arrival to power of an Ultra government, an event
alleged to be longed for by the whole country, could save
the situation.   Unfortunately a certain amount of colour was
given to his picture of woe by the Bonapartist conspiracy at

Grenoble in May ; though Didier, a political adventurer who had tried everything in turn from revolution to royalism, did not rally more than about a thousand followers to his standard. But General Donnadieu, the commanding-officer of the district, made a good story out of the whole affair in order to glorify himself, and reported to Paris that the rebels numbered at least 4000. The government, therefore, thinking that it was faced with a serious rebellion, gave wide discretionary powers to the local authorities, and a reign of terror followed in Isère as the rising was stamped out with unnecessary brutality. This caused a great wave of feeling in the whole country against the Ultras and against the *Chambre introuvable* in particular.

The allied Powers had, for some time, been viewing with growing anxiety the activities of this militant chamber, which in January 1816 had tried to bring about the overthrow of the ministry by a violent attack on the budget proposals. Richelieu wrote to Osmond in London that the ministry's successors were already designated, among them Jules de Polignac and Hyde de Neuville—two of the most rampant Ultras, the former of whom was to have the supreme distinction, fourteen years later, of being the chief instrument in bringing his master's crown rolling into the dust. The Duke of Wellington, said Richelieu, was behaving splendidly at this time, and was more friendly than one could have thought him capable of being ; but what a melancholy thing it was to be supported in one's own country only by foreigners. Richelieu constantly speaks in his correspondence of Wellington's friendly and sympathetic understanding of his difficulties at this period (the episode of the back interest on reclamations had yet to come), in sharp contrast to the British Ambassador, Sir Charles Stuart, self-sufficient, intriguing and jealous of his colleagues, particularly of Pozzo di Borgo. The unfortunate Richelieu, owing to his friendship with the Tsar and Pozzo, was a special target for the British Ambassador's animosity ; to such an extent that, after many bitter complaints in correspondence of Stuart's ill manners, the duke was reduced to the state where, as Osmond was informed, " My flesh creeps every time he comes in." Yet both Castlereagh and Wellington were agreed that in the existing state of European affairs, Richelieu's Russian connection was actually an important asset to the stability of France, and Castlereagh impressed on the unwilling Stuart that so long as Richelieu continued to pursue a moderate policy, his ministry must be given every support, since " whatever errors of management on his part there may have been, there appears to have been none in intention. He acts with honour and good faith. He is above tricks, and in the present demoralised state of France if he falls I don't know how the King can replace him."

To Langeron, Richelieu wrote that the parliamentary crisis which must surely lead in a few weeks to the fall of his ministry would bring him his " deliverance." Yet he would not at once feel able to return to Odessa, much as he would like to do so, since he had now torn up all his roots there ; besides, after leaving the Russian service for the French, he could not turn about so soon and leave the French service again for the Russian. What he would like to do would be to travel east across Europe, avoiding the large towns, through Switzerland and Italy to Greece and Constantinople, finally arriving in Odessa as a private individual, to see once more the beloved coasts, and all the trees he had planted.

But the hour of release was not yet. Both the Tsar and the Austrian Emperor conveyed their alarm at the political situation in France through their ambassadors to Louis XVIII and to Richelieu. It was not easy, however, to bring either the King or his chief minister to the point of taking so decisive a step as dissolution of the Chamber, notwithstanding the pressure being applied from Russian quarters through the medium of Pozzo di Borgo. " After all," said Richelieu to Decazes, " they are Royalists. One must govern for them, and in spite of them, if that is necessary. They must be saved in spite of themselves." To Richelieu it was indeed unthinkable that the restored monarchy could remain on a durable foundation without the support of the nobility, and he recoiled from taking any step which could cause an irreconcilable break with the Royalists. The King was equally reluctant to take such a final step against the Chamber which he had at first hailed with great satisfaction. But when Richelieu had himself come to see that the Chamber must go, he wrote to Decazes to say that he had been strongly urging that course on the King, he thought to some effect, and he asked Decazes to find out from Lainé the proper form of the necessary ordinance, that they might lose no time in drawing one up for the King to sign. Yet even the concerted efforts of Decazes, Pasquier, Royer-Collard and Molé, supported as they were in the end by Lainé, Corvetto and Richelieu, might not have sufficed to bring Louis XVIII to a decision but for the personal letters of warning he had received both from the Tsar and from Wellington. When the fateful decision had at last been taken, Monsieur was not informed until the King had safely retired to bed on the evening of the 5th September. Richelieu then told him that the ordinance had been signed, and would be published in the *Moniteur* the following day. Monsieur, beside himself with anger and astonishment, was only restrained from going straight to his brother by Richelieu's reminder that the King by that time would be asleep and had expressly forbidden anyone to waken him. Monsieur's sons, however, who whatever their faults had considerably more sense than their father, did not share his anger, but on the contrary openly approved of the King's action. Paris, too, as a whole received the news well. Richelieu was given a tremendous ovation when he attended the Opera on the evening following the publication of the ordinance, and he wrote to the Marquis d'Osmond that there had been an appreciable rise in government stocks ; " but the *salons* are furious, and I am not fit to be thrown to the dogs." As for M. de Bruges, busily spreading his tales of woe in English political circles, the news took him by surprise and placed him in a distinctly difficult position ; so that he who the night before had been saying that only a change of government could save France, now found himself obliged to turn about and prophesy that elections would mean civil war.

Unfortunately, however, he did succeed in planting some alarm in government circles in England, so that there was a stiffening in the attitude of the British Government which was reflected in that of Wellington when he returned to Paris. Richelieu wrote to the Tsar on the 15th October : " I shall try to bring back the Duke of Wellington to an opinion which was his a couple of months ago, and which events since taking place have only strengthened. I will own that I very much fear that instructions have come from London to check his goodwill towards us, for it is impossible for me to raise the least doubt upon the straightforwardness and integrity of his character." Richelieu also had several conversations on the subject with Canning, who was then visiting Paris, but the English statesman was not to be drawn into committing himself to any definite pronouncement ; the best that Richelieu could report about their talks was that Canning was not able to give a single good reason why the size of the occupying armies should not be reduced. Wellington took his stand upon the fact that Prussia had not yet been consulted on the matter. Prussia, when consulted, was difficult. When at last a definite pronouncement could be extracted from Berlin, it was the uncompromising statement that reduction of the army of occupation would be an effect, not a cause, and that when Prussia could see the French Chambers working in accord with the government, she would give her decision.

Disappointed but not defeated, Richelieu then laid the question before the Ambassadors' Conference, where he was supported as usual by Pozzo di Borgo. He also wrote to Wellington on the 17th October, asking for a reduction in the size of the army of occupation by 30,000 men, to which reduction he declared that Austria and Russia had already consented. He concluded with the persuasive argument that it would be a powerful impulse to the opening of the new Chamber if the King in his speech were able to make such a favourable announcement. This suggestion, however, was not received by Wellington with any great enthusiasm. He replied that he was sorry not to be of the same opinion ; he feared that Richelieu had been misinformed about the views of the Powers on the subject, and he pointed out that the same people who were now expressing eagerness for the departure of the allied troops were precisely those who only a year before had been crying out to him " You are not going to leave the King and his family in the hands of these assassins ? "

Soon after this, Wellington was recalled to London for further consultations, and when he returned in the New Year, the situation in France had somewhat improved. Negotiations had been opened through the good offices of Ouvrard with the bankers Hope and Baring, and it seemed that their assistance would go far towards clearing a way through France's financial thickets (though resort to the English bankers appears to have caused a certain degree of professional jealousy in the house of Rothschild, and Richelieu was made conscious of a distinct chill in his relations with its members). Hope and Baring were not willing to cover more than 200 of the 300 millions required, but the French bankers were at last induced to come forward and put up the rest, while a chastened Chamber actually voted the necessary 30 millions of *rentes*. Wellington therefore was now willing to agree to a reduction of 30,000 men, and this was officially decided upon at a conference on the 10th February, 1817, by which time the Hope-Baring loan had been launched.

Richelieu had thus achieved his immediate objective in an appreciable reduction of the allied forces in France, but he had not lost sight of his final aim : the total ending of the foreign occupation. His task was not rendered any easier by the attempt made in Paris in the spring of 1818 to assassinate Wellington, an incident which not unnaturally gave the intended victim a poorer opinion than ever of conditions in

France ; but Richelieu continued to press for complete evacuation, despite the continued efforts of the Ultras to pull in the opposite direction. Their next manœuvre was the drawing up of the memorandum known as the Secret Note, which was sent out in July 1818 to the principal foreign ministers in Paris just a month before the meeting of the allied Powers at the Congress of Aix-la-Chapelle. Though the continuation of the occupation was not directly asked for in so many words, the note represented France as a smouldering volcano of revolution, whose eruption could only be avoided by a change of government. Vitrolles, the ostensible author of this document, could well have been put on trial for treason, but for certain delicate reasons mentioned by Pasquier in his memoirs : " It would have been necessary to have produced proof that he was the author of the anonymous document, to have been quite sure that he had not communicated his memorandum to the very highly placed personage who honoured him with his protection." Vitrolles was, however, deprived of his office as Minister of State and his political career was broken until his master succeeded to the throne ; while Richelieu produced a memorandum replying specifically to the allegations contained in the note and stressing the calm reigning throughout the country.

Wellington, though now taking a rather less gloomy view of French affairs, was not yet prepared to go as far as complete evacuation of French territory. But within the ensuing twelve months, circumstances gradually forced him to a change of opinion. With the rising tide of friction between the occupying troops and the inhabitants of the country, he began to perceive the strategic perils of having his troops scattered about an increasingly hostile country. In a memorandum to the British cabinet, he advised gathering the allied armies into a belt between the Scheldt and the Meuse, where they would not be in danger of being taken unawares and overwhelmed by a sudden rising. In the face of this expert advice the British Government was brought over on to the side of immediate evacuation. As for Austria, in her alarm at Russia's pro-French attitude which she suspected of paving the way toward the much-dreaded Franco-Russian alliance, she had been ready to pronounce for evacuation as early as September 1816, and it was Britain who at that time restrained her. As far as the liberation of French territory was concerned, therefore, Richelieu's cause was already won before the actual meeting of the Congress of Aix-la-Chapelle, the final act of the Vienna peace-making, which was to be held " to take into consideration, in concert with His Most Christian Majesty, the internal condition of France and to decide thereafter whether the occupation of the frontier provinces of the kingdom could cease or whether it ought to be continued."

The Congress assembled in the autumn of 1818 at Aix-la-Chapelle. The ancient capital of Charlemagne and of his Holy Roman Empire could seldom even in its long history have contained a gathering of so many notables as on this occasion : the Emperors of Russia and Austria, the King of Prussia, their respective ministers Nesselrode, Metternich and Hardenberg ; the British delegation headed by Castlereagh and Wellington, the latter attending in the double capacity of British plenipotentiary and commander-in-chief of the occupying forces ; while Richelieu attended as the chief representative of France, bringing with him Rayneval, the head of his Foreign Ministerial chancellery, and Baron Mounier. Among the many others present, in addition to the inevitable Pozzo di Borgo, were the bankers Hope and Baring, together with the Viennese member of the house of Rothschild ; the Empress Dowager of Russia and various German royalties who had come to view the proceedings as spectators, and finally, Sir Thomas Lawrence, the most celebrated portrait painter of the day. The latter had been specially commissioned to make portraits of all the prominent people attending the Congress, since the Prince Regent wished to have a complete portrait collection of all those associated with the peace settlement of Europe. The original plan had been for Lawrence to attend the Congress of Vienna for this purpose, but the intervention of the Hundred Days had put a stop to the arrangement. For the Congress of Aix, the British Government provided Lawrence with a specially constructed studio of wood, at a cost of over a thousand pounds, which was to be sent out to him there. But sad to relate, it never got farther than the port of Antwerp, and Lawrence worked instead in a gallery of the Town Hall placed at his disposal by the resourceful municipality of Aix. Amongst the many fine portraits he produced, that of Richelieu was considered an excellent likeness, and six copies of it were made for the benefit of the duke's family.

Before setting out for the Congress, Richelieu spent a few days at Courteilles, whose pleasant and peaceful countryside, he declared, had only one drawback : it made him long for a less unnatural mode of life than that he was obliged to lead in Paris. But such thoughts must be firmly put aside, in view of the great task that lay immediately ahead of him. On his way to Aix, Richelieu paused for three days at Spa, in order to have time for some preliminary discussions with Castlereagh. His instructions for the Congress emphatically laid down that the two matters which must have priority were the evacuation of French territory and the breaking of the quadruple alliance against France. He found the British Foreign Secretary most amenable on the points which in fact had been already decided, but the knotty problem of France and the Alliance was a different matter.

However, agreement having been already reached on the question of evacuation, the official announcement to that effect was issued on 9th October. When the news reached Paris, there was a great outburst of popular rejoicing. For once, all shades of opinion in the Press were united in praise of Richelieu, while the King wrote that he had lived long enough, now that he could behold France free and her flag flying once more over all French towns.

But when at the Congress Richelieu attempted to broach the subject of France's future relations with the Alliance, the temperature grew cool. Indeed he found himself making so little progress that when on 25th October, Castlereagh brought up such matters as the slave trade and the proposed maritime league against the Barbary pirates, Richelieu replied that much as he would like to discuss these subjects, if there were any question of signing an agreement it would be impossible for him to attach his signature unless he could first be informed of his exact status in the gathering and of France's position with regard to the other four Powers. To the King he wrote that there was no need to worry about the maritime league, since he was quite sure that it would have advanced no further by the end of another two years ! But as for " Milord Castlereagh," the English statesman appeared to be in continual fear of his Parliament ; at the same time, however, Richelieu darkly suspected that there was a secret under-standing between England and Austria.

But soon after this unpromising beginning, the Tsar arrived, and Richelieu lost no time in directing his appeals to the Russian sovereign, with whom he had a conversation lasting two hours. Yet even here the results were dis-appointing. Alexander referred once again to the unstable condition of France and to the necessity which therefore still existed, and would continue to exist after the evacuation, of the Powers standing together in alliance to ensure the maintenance of peace. He was uneasy about the permanence of the Bourbon régime ; they had done themselves great damage, he declared, by their treatment of former imperial functionaries and soldiers, who had been thrown into opposi-tion and were turning to plots as a way out of an intolerable situation. The Tsar professed his own willingness to receive the King into the Alliance, but intimated that he could not go against Castlereagh.

The Powers at Aix were, in fact, divided into two schools of thought : those who wished France to take part in the deliberations of the old Quadruple Alliance merely as an invited guest, and those who followed the plan put forward by the Tsar, of a general alliance in which not only France but other states would be included to watch over the peace of Europe. Castlereagh was opposed to the Russian plan, but he favoured the inclusion of France in the periodical reunions of Powers provided for in the Second Peace of Paris. (Though Lord Liverpool, agitated at the idea of admitting France to the Alliance, was writing to Castlereagh that such a proposal would split the British cabinet.) Metternich, with his customary agility, steered a middle course : since France could not be left in isolation and since the Quadruple Alliance existed and must continue to exist, France must somehow be linked to it. As October drew towards its end, the matter still remained unsettled while the Tsar and the King of Prussia, at Richelieu's urgent prompting, paid a short visit to Paris. There Alexander had a long talk with Louis XVIII, who had been previously warned by Richelieu that he must not appear to be angling for an alliance. On the 31st October the two sovereigns returned to Aix and discussions were resumed. The Tsar showed signs of reverting to his cherished scheme for a general alliance, but a hastily summoned meeting of all the ministers succeeded in restraining him from straying down that perilous path, and in mid-November, two pro-tocols were finally issued. The first of these, which was communicated privately to Richelieu, maintained the Quad-ruple Alliance ; but the second published the association of France with the union of the four Powers, and was to be made known to all the states which had been signatories of the peace treaties.

Thus, at last, was France admitted to the Quadruple Alliance. Castlereagh and Metternich hoped by this means to prevent her from falling into the arms of Russia ; but Richelieu wrote to Louis XVIII : " It is owing to the Emperor of Russia and to his all-powerful intervention, that we have attained the end which for the last four weeks seemed always to elude us."

With the successful outcome of his three years' struggle for the restoration of France to her place among the European Powers, Richelieu hurried home from Aix in November, to be back in Paris in time for the re-opening of the Chambers and to face the fresh troubles awaiting him there, where events had come to a head as a result of the autumn elections. Needless to say, and as Mme de Montcalm remarks with some bitterness in her Journal, no word of credit or of gratitude for his achievements was given to Richelieu by the Ultras or their prince, although the King conferred upon him the cross of the Order of the Holy Ghost. But the Ultras' mouthpiece, Chateaubriand, who had failed to enlist Richelieu's support for his efforts to regain the monarch's favour, was at pains to pay fulsome tribute for the results of Aix to " the wisdom of the King " and the moderation of the allied sovereigns.

CHAPTER VI

EXIT THE MINISTRY

THOUGH the dissolution of the *Chambre introuvable* in the autumn of 1816 had swept many of the most rampant Ultras from the Chamber, it had by no means solved all the ministry's difficulties. The Left, in which Republicans and Bonapartists had by this time joined hands, was becoming increasingly vocal and hostile to the government. This was all the more alarming since the new electoral law of 1817, the work of Decazes and the Doctrinaires Guizot, Royer-Collard and Barante, and which would be in force for the first time in the coming elections of 1818, would bring into action a large middle-class electorate. This would no doubt act as a check on the extreme Royalists, but it would at the same time provide an extremely strong reinforcement to the numbers of the Left.

Moreover, the rifts in the cabinet itself had deepened, and had split it into two distinct halves : one headed by Decazes and Gouvion St. Cyr whose leaning was towards the moderate Left, and who were supported by the Doctrinaires ; the other led by Richelieu and Lainé (who had succeeded Vaublanc as Minister of the Interior in May 1816). These last two, especially Richelieu, viewed with increasing dismay the resurgence and mounting activity of the Left. Convinced as he was of the necessity of Royalist support for the proper functioning of the King's government, Richelieu felt that the cabinet ought to try and draw closer to the Right, notwithstanding the fact that a certain number of Ultras, in their spite against the ministry, were making common cause with the Left. At the beginning of 1818, Richelieu wrote bitterly to the Tsar's minister Capodistrias : " It is indeed strange enough to see men who pretend to be exclusively Royalist unite themselves to the most ardent Republicans, and through hatred of the ministers whom they detest, vote for all the most anti-monarchic proposals that are suggested to them. This double opposition, which some of the Doctrinaires have joined, puts us in a very difficult position and could finally bring the government to a standstill."

Not only were some of the Ultras making common cause with their natural enemies of the Left, but in their search for implements to use in the overthrow of the ministry they had not lost sight of Talleyrand. That veteran diplomat, who had so well chosen the moment for his retreat from office, had however not counted on being left in retirement indefinitely, and as time went on, his irritation at the continued neglect of his talents mounted until it could no longer be kept within the bounds of decorum. Richelieu, he sneered, was the Tsar's liege man, incapable of having any will of his own or of upholding the dignity and independence of his country abroad. Such remarks, while not achieving their main purpose, unfortunately did Richelieu considerable harm in the eyes of the French public, especially in ill-informed provincial circles. Talleyrand's spite was also directed against Decazes, whose removal was declared to be as necessary as that of Richelieu. Talleyrand's tirades reached a climax with his violent attack on Decazes at a British Embassy dinner, at which he expressed himself with such spiteful violence about the royal favourite that for a time he was deprived of his office of Grand Chamberlain and banished from Court.

As a matter of fact, Richelieu's own relations with Decazes had by this time become a little strained. Now that Decazes had made a brilliant marriage with the daughter of the Comte de Saint-Aulaire, both he and his wife's relations felt that the post of Minister of Police was unworthy of him, and that he should have the portfolio of the Ministry of the Interior. Fouché had given an ugly sound to the title of Minister of Police, and moreover it was an office which was hardly in keeping with the idea of constitutional government. But Richelieu had no intention of sacrificing his Minister of the Interior, Lainé, who if not brilliant was a man of integrity and moderate views—which he had had the courage to maintain even during his administrative service throughout the period of the Revolution and the Empire.

Before the Congress of Aix-la-Chapelle, Richelieu, utterly disheartened by the endless political warfare of which he found himself the unwilling centre, had begun once again to contemplate retiring, and before actually starting on his journey to the Congress he announced to the King his intention of doing so as soon as the Congress was over. He wrote to the Abbé Nicolle in a similar vein, saying that the final attainment of the evacuation of French territory would be the moment for his " Nunc dimittis " and for the rest which he so badly needed ; the parliamentary session following the Congress should see the end of his political career. France, he added, had made astonishing progress during the previous twelve months, and if only she would behave sensibly, she had within herself all the ingredients of the most astonishing prosperity. But her future would depend on herself and her own behaviour. Decazes now advised Louis XVIII to appeal to the Tsar, begging him to try and prevail on the duke to reconsider his decision to retire. The King wrote to Wellington, who was already at Aix, asking him to enlist Alexander's support and influence. Wellington, in reply, spoke of his hope " that the Emperor's intervention will preserve to Your Majesty the services of a minister whose loyal character has contributed so much to conciliate all the interests of Europe with those of France." He showed the King's letter to the Tsar, who promised to do what he could. When Alexander paid a brief visit to Paris during the Congress he told Louis XVIII what he had said to Richelieu : " You think that you have now discharged your duty towards your country ; but you are not yet freed from it. You have just gone through three stormy years, but France and Europe need you for another three. You do not believe yourself

fitted for the management of the Chambers : very well, you
have got M. Decazes who is excellent in that respect ; M.
Lainé is also very good. Use them, but do not desert your
post." As a result of these exhortations, Richelieu for the
time being dropped the idea of retirement. But with each
fresh discouragement in the political situation at home, it
would rise again to the foreground of his mind.

The results of the elections were declared while Richelieu
was still at Aix-la-Chapelle. He had warned both the King
and Decazes that in the eyes of Europe the election results
would be a test of the stability of France, and though the
results did not realise all the hopes of Decazes, they more
than confirmed the worst fears of Richelieu and of the allied
sovereigns at Aix when they heard of the nomination of
Lafayette, Manuel and Benjamin Constant. Richelieu saw
the time rapidly approaching when there would be a Liberal
majority which nothing but a *coup d'état* would be able to
defeat. " I see our future as black," he wrote to Decazes,
" and mine as in the most sombre colours ; for if things go
badly, there will be no means of getting out, and to remain
would be for me a hundred times worse than to die." Decazes,
however, without replying to these gloomy comments, merely
answered that " We need to see each other to come to an
understanding and arrange what we are to do. It is urgent
that you should return as soon as possible." A few days
later, Richelieu in a fresh wave of pessimism wrote : " I shall
return to France with a shrinking of the heart in foreseeing
all the ills that threaten this unfortunate country. The
liberty of the Press is a Pandora's box from which come forth
all the calamities which desolate the earth. With it, all ancient
institutions are destroyed and the new ones do not take root.
The Duke of Wellington predicted it to me long ago." Just
before his actual departure from Aix, Richelieu wrote again
to Decazes : " Let us think no more of liberal concessions.
We have made enough, and much good they have done us."
Again he speaks of retirement, which draws forth an imploring
protest from Decazes.

The new session of the Chamber opened on the 10th December, with the cabinet if possible even more deeply divided than before. Decazes, attacked once more by the Ultras from the first moment of the new session, strongly opposed any further approach to them, whereas Molé now came out openly in support of Richelieu and Lainé. But Richelieu's proposal to alter the new electoral law by restoring to the district electoral assemblies, which were dominated by the landed aristocracy, their former right to nominate electors in the second degree, horrified and alienated the Doctrinaires. They now broke away altogether from the government, and with a complete reversal of their previous attitude proceeded to take the side of the Chamber against the King's ministers. The question of the electoral law also roused the opposition of Pasquier and St. Cyr, with the latter of whom Richelieu, who had never approved of the Marshal's military law, was already in strong disagreement over the proposed increase in the war budget. Harassed and disgusted by the intrigues of Decazes on the one hand manœuvring for position with the threat of resignation employed as a weapon of coercion, while on the other, Monsieur did not cease to pull his hidden strings, Richelieu longed to resign. But he hesitated to do so, in the certainty that the only alternative choice for the King would be the detested Talleyrand. Lainé, holding the portfolio of the Interior for which Decazes was angling, was threatening in his turn to resign, and was only restrained from doing so in the knowledge that he would thereby let in Decazes, with his dangerous Liberal tendencies. Richelieu felt that if Lainé went, he himself would certainly not feel able to remain ; yet on the other hand, if he resigned, Talleyrand would inevitably step in. But at last it became clear to the duke that whatever the consequences of his retirement, it had become impossible for his cabinet to continue to function under the existing circumstances, and he therefore hesitated no longer in submitting his resignation to the King. Decazes promptly begged that the King would accept his own resignation—" Nothing in the world would

ÉLIE, DUC DECAZES

persuade me to remain in the ministry a moment after the Duc de Richelieu "—and the rest of the cabinet lost no time in following their leader's example.

But then followed agitated negotiations in an attempt to make Richelieu withdraw his resignation. Decazes, in order to demonstrate that he bore the duke no ill will, was the first to take action, appealing to the Tsar's minister Nesselrode, who happened at that moment to be in Paris. The King himself suffered almost as much nervous wear and tear as his ministers, since, while he did not wish to lose Richelieu when Talleyrand was waiting to step into the duke's shoes, he wished even less that Decazes should lose a foothold in the cabinet. He therefore struggled for days to find some compromise. But Richelieu would only contemplate returning on condition that Lainé remained with him and that Decazes was sent right away. Decazes offered to retire to his property at La Grave for three months ; Richelieu, however, wrote to the King : " Your Majesty knows how I like and estime M. Decazes ; my feelings are, and always will be, the same. But assailed without cause on the one hand by a party whose extravagances have caused so much trouble, it is impossible for him to come to an understanding with them ; on the other hand, pushed towards a party whose doctrines menace us still more, so long as he is not settled outside France in some important position, all those opposed to the ministry will look upon him as the focal point of their hopes, and he will become, no doubt unwillingly, an obstruction to government." Repugnant though it was to use such language to the King, pursued Richelieu, it was his duty to tell His Majesty the truth as he saw it, and if the government was to function at all, then he saw nothing for it but for Decazes to be sent as ambassador to either Naples or St. Petersburg, and that within the ensuing week. Richelieu at first had tried to compromise by agreeing that Decazes should retreat " provisionally " as far as Leghorn, but later, censured by both Molé and Villèle, and worked on, it was suspected, by Pozzo di Borgo, his attitude hardened and he insisted that this would not be enough, but that Decazes must go to Russia; which cruel ultimatum was accepted and duly transmitted, mingled with the royal tears, to Decazes. However, Lainé represented to Richelieu that to send Decazes as far away as Russia would be to make a martyr of him; it would be better to let him go to La Grave. Richelieu saw this point, and finally agreed. He then set to work to fulfil his part of the bargain by reconstructing the cabinet minus the Ministry of Police, which office was then suppressed.

But at once fresh difficulties arose. St. Cyr, Roy and Pasquier declared that they would not remain without Decazes. Even Lainé was seized with scruples over his part in the electoral-law discussions. In short, by Christmas Day Richelieu's proposed combination had fallen to pieces, while the duke was rapidly worrying himself into one of his usual states of nervous prostration. He wrote to the Tsar: " I have done everything in my power to avoid having to go out of office, and if I have at last resolved to retire, it is in the firm conviction that I can no longer do any good in it." Richelieu could only suggest to the King now that he should call on some of the marshals or peers, for example Macdonald or Marmont, who were at least harmless and had some knowledge both of the country and of the army. Louis XVIII, therefore, decided to call on General Desolles ; but the Comte de Serre and Baron Louis, who were to take the portfolios of Justice and Finance in the new ministry, insisted that Decazes could not be passed over. At last, therefore, though with a suitable show of reluctance, Decazes obtained the long-desired portfolio of the Interior.

Thinking over in later years the events of 1818, the Duc de Broglie, Mme de Staël's son-in-law, frankly admits that the part played by his friends the Doctrinaires and the moderate Liberals in the overthrow of Richelieu's first ministry was a lamentable mistake. To have found, under the very difficult circumstances of the Restoration, a man of the character and integrity of Richelieu, with a cabinet containing such men as

Pasquier, Molé and Corvetto, who were able to use in the service of the new régime the long administrative experience acquired under the vigilant eye of Napoleon, was an unparalleled piece of good fortune, not to be lightly cast away. Moreover, whatever its shortcomings, the ministry could show a considerable measure of achievement : in addition to the duke's outstanding work for the liberation and reinstatement of France, the national finances had been overhauled under the capable management of Corvetto, and a new accounting system established. With the aid of the powerful support of the house of Baring, the credit of France had been restored and placed on the solid foundations upon which it was to remain for a century ; even by 1818 her finances were on a sounder basis than any other country in Europe save England. Yet all this was to count for nothing when weighed in the scales of party conflict, and as Broglie laments, the ministry was overturned for the sake of maintaining an electoral law which, although good in principle, was far from perfect in detail and did, in fact, justify some of Richelieu's fears. As for the Royalists for whose support he had never ceased to work, it was through no lack of effort on their part, as we have seen, that Richelieu's ministry was not brought to the ground a good deal earlier.

CHAPTER VII

ESCAPE TO FREEDOM

ALTHOUGH Richelieu was now no longer a member of the government, it soon became clear that he had not ceased to be a target for the spite and rancour of political parties.

It was known that his sole revenue now was the 10,000 francs which was his salary as First Gentleman of the Bed-chamber, and on the 30th December 1818, the Marquis de Lally-Tollendal in the Upper House and the deputy, Benjamin Delessert in the Lower House, brought forward proposals praying the King to assign to Richelieu a suitable reward " proportionate to the eminence of his services and his dis-interested impartiality, worthy both of the satisfaction of his King and the gratitude of a great nation." The two proposals having been carried almost unanimously, the cabinet brought forward a project in January to confer upon Richelieu a pension of 50,000 francs to be attached to his peerage and to be passed on in due course to his heirs.

But immediately the opposition, both of Right and Left, were up in arms, the most violent resistance coming from the very Royalists whom the duke had been so anxious to conciliate. A former member of the *Chambre introuvable*, Kergolay, surpassed others in the personal venom of his attack, alleging that Richelieu had not by his talents earned any title to a national gift ; while a Liberal peer, Lanjuinais, had the effrontery to declare that Richelieu was in a state of opulence and had no need of any money. When the duke himself had heard of the first proposals brought forward in the Chambers, his reaction was to refuse any proffered gift : he did not wish, he said, to be the means of laying a further financial burden on the nation, which was already saddled with an enormous load of debt. Too many calamities had befallen the country, too many of its citizens had fallen on hard times and there were too many losses to be made good, for him to see his fortune built up at such a moment. " The esteem of my country, the goodwill of the King, the testimony of my own conscience are sufficient." However, in spite of the duke's words, the Chambers in their first enthusiasm had gone ahead with the proposals, which had now become the occasion for an exhibition of mean-spirited party rancour hard to surpass. Courvoisier finally presented an amendment proposing that the grant should last only for the continuance of the direct line of the duke's family. It was pointed out in vain by Saint-Aulaire and Delessert that as Richelieu had no children, this proposal would take away all real value from the award ; the amendment was carried by a huge majority.

Richelieu, cut to the heart by the whole affair, decided that he would not touch any of the money so grudgingly awarded ; " There is no great merit in this little sacrifice," he wrote to his old friend, the Marquis de Vérac, " since they have deprived me of the power of leaving the money to my nephew, which alone would have made it worth having." He decided to donate the entire sum to the foundation of a new hospital at Bordeaux, a town having links with his family, since his grandfather had been Governor of Guyenne ; besides which, Bordeaux was the one French town which had rendered a real service to the royal cause by calling the Duc d'Angoulême within its walls in 1814. But Richelieu wished his donation to be kept as quiet as possible.

Decazes, however, who in spite of their political differences, remained on very good terms with the duke, did him a real service by getting the King to appoint Richelieu to the office of Master of the Royal Hunt, a sinecure carrying a salary which through the good offices of Decazes was raised to 50,000 francs, and which entailed no tiresome duties about the Court such as were attendant on being First Gentleman of the Bedchamber—or First Equerry, another post which Decazes had previously offered to Richelieu. The life of a

Court functionary was one whose prospect the duke simply
could not face. As he wrote to Decazes, it would have been
for him at any time a nightmare : " I could not have stood
it, I should have tendered my resignation, and that would
have produced a bad effect that I should prefer to avoid. If
then the King is willing to let me have this office of Master
of the Hunt he will give me great pleasure. I give my word
of honour not to interfere with anything ; that will reassure
the princes, and my place will be fixed for ever. You see
how frankly I speak to you and how I count on your friendship. You know how much of this it is suitable to tell the
King and on how much to keep silent. I trust to you."
There was one slight difficulty about the appointment : the
house used for the residence of the Master of the Royal Hunt
happened to be occupied, and the occupant refused to move.
It required all the efforts of the Intendant of Crown Lands,
backed by the Minister of the Interior, to eject him.

But when this had been at last achieved, Léon de Rochechouart was as usual charged with the task of getting the
duke's household established—which process, he was carefully instructed, " must not be ruinous. Anyway, I shall
economise as much as I can, in order to have enough to set
myself up and give some balls." For released at last from
the thankless burden which had hung about his neck like a
millstone for three years, Richelieu could now look forward
once more to the enjoyment of a normal social life. " Like
a boy out of school," as Mme de Montcalm expressed it, he
decided to go off on a tour of the Midi, in an attempt to
restore his health ; for he was far from well after all the
stresses and strains of the previous three years. He took
with him his former aide-de-camp, Colonel Stempkowski,
whom the Tsar had allowed to remain with Richelieu during
the years of the occupation by being attached to the Russian
forces in France ; Stempkowski was now on leave till the end
of the summer before returning to Russia. Richelieu left Paris
on the 4th January 1819, with the firm intention of remaining
well away from the capital for at least several months.

Before actually going south, he and Stempowski went to pay a visit to Courteilles, which Richelieu had now commenced to visit frequently, stopping usually at Tremblay on his way in order to take the Marquis de Vérac along with him. On this occasion, Richelieu and Stempkowski remained at Courteilles for about a fortnight ; then on the 20th January they set out for Bordeaux, where the duke planned to spend about nine days. From there he wrote to Vérac that he was happy and contented in his new idleness, that he was gently renewing his acquaintance with the beautiful countryside of France and taking great pleasure in it. He reported that the most perfect peace reigned everywhere, in spite of the malevolent influence of the opposition Press, which was corrupting even Bordeaux, that stronghold of royalism. During his stay at Bordeaux, Richelieu spent three days exploring the Landes on horseback, writing to Rochechouart afterwards that he had seen many things of interest in a country " so savage that the steppe is nothing to it." From Bordeaux he went on to Toulouse, Montpellier and Nimes, being received everywhere with an enthusiasm which, as he confessed in confidence to Vérac, he began to find rather wearisome. " I cannot put my nose out of doors," he wrote, " without little urchins running after me." He hoped, he added, that he would not be received at his next stop as he had been at Montpellier, where General Briche had insisted on escorting him through the town, complete with Mme Briche and a squadron of Chasseurs— " I did not know where to bury myself," said the poor duke. From Nimes he wrote to Vérac that his repugnance at the idea of a return to Paris was growing daily, especially since he had learned of all the unpleasantness to which his poor sisters had been subjected over the " wretched affair " of his award. When he finally reached Marseilles, he found everything extraordinarily peaceful, as elsewhere in the Midi. "You would not believe," he wrote to Vérac, " how little impression is made here by all those discussions which have so much agitated the *salons* of Paris. I can assure you that to change or not to change the electoral law is all the same to the vast majority of Frenchmen."

While Richelieu was in Marseilles, he received a very friendly letter from the Tsar, who announced that he was about to visit the provinces of New-Russia, and invited Richelieu pressingly to come and join him. But much as he would have liked to go, the duke wrote to Rochechouart, it must not be yet. The situation in Paris at that time was becoming increasingly tense, with the presentation to the Chamber of two great measures of reform : the Doctrinaires' great bill for the freedom of the Press, and the equally daring electoral reform proposals put forward by the Comte de Serre. Richelieu observes that he feels there must be an explosion soon, and he must not, therefore, appear to be deserting France in her hour of need. " But keep calm," he writes, " I shall not be minister ; no power on earth is capable of making me return to the ministry." Brave words ! . . .

Richelieu had not forgotten or lost interest in New-Russia, however. In the midst of all the worries of his first ministry, and even during the Congress of Aix-la-Chapelle, he had found time to correspond with Russian ministers as well as with the Tsar himself over various matters particularly close to his heart : his proposal to make Odessa into a free port, the welfare of the Odessa Lycée which now bore his name and of the twenty pupils for whose education he was paying with the pension awarded to him by the Tsar. Russian bureaucracy had tried to stop this pension after his return to France, and he had had to appeal to the Tsar, who issued a new rescript. At other times, Richelieu had sent to Odessa seeds and fruit-tree cuttings from the King's gardens, or worked for the introduction of French merchandise into New-Russia. During the grain shortage of 1816, he was responsible for bringing Black Sea grain supplies to France. He never ceased to lament in his letters to friends his pain at the separation from Odessa and his hope that he would soon be in a position to revisit it. When the Emperor Alexander toured the Black Sea coast and saw for himself the work that Richelieu had done there, he marked his gratitude by sending the duke an autograph letter together with the Grand Cordon of the Order of St. Andrew. He also caused a bust of the duke to be set up in the Lycée at Odessa, showing him crowned with evergreens and bearing the inscription : " To Richelieu : grateful Odessa."

In the meantime, Richelieu continued his tour by way of the Riviera coast from Hyères to Nice along the Corniche road, a region which he was very interested to compare with the Crimea. He found the land more cultivated than in Russia, but he did not find any place equal to his beloved Urzuov, either for sheer beauty of situation or for luxuriance of vegetation. He thought it a pity that the Corniche road, begun by Napoleon, had not as yet been finished : " our departments of the Midi would have greatly profited." The two travellers continued along the Mediterranean coast to Genoa, with whose appearance and fine buildings Richelieu was greatly impressed ; it was small wonder, he concluded, that a people with such a past did not want to be just a province of Piedmont.

From Genoa they went on to Leghorn, where they had the great pleasure of meeting their old friend Sicard ; we can imagine at what length the affairs of Odessa were discussed. It appeared that trade was not good at that time in the port, since there had been a succession of abundant harvests in Europe after the previous bad years, while in France the country landowners were asking for higher tariffs against the imported grain for which they had been grateful enough during the lean times.

After his stay in Genoa, the duke turned north on his way to the Italian lakes, passing through Florence, Bologna, Ferrara, Venice and Milan. From Florence he wrote to Rochechouart in May 1819 that his health was still not good ; his nerves had now recovered, but he was suffering from continual gastric troubles. However, these do not seem in any way to have impaired his astounding reserve of energy, and he admits that he does not find the journey tiring. In fact, after making a tour round Lakes Como and Maggiore, he writes to the Marquis de Vérac from Milan in very good

spirits : " I have just made a charming trip which has given
me back all my inclination to travel. I find Europe so small
and communications so rapid that I do not know why people
do not give themselves the pleasure of travelling about it,
especially when they have at several points, persons with
whom they have old links of affection. One must have a
central point to establish one's nest (for me this would be
Paris), then from there one can take flight as easily to the
north as to the south." Obviously, there was nothing like
touring about the steppes of southern Russia to give one a
proper perspective of distances and ease of travel in early
nineteenth-century Europe. The duke then put his precepts
into practice by crossing the Simplon Pass and making a
fairly extensive tour of Switzerland. He had written to
Rochechouart, before leaving Italy, asking him to buy two
fine saddle horses, if necessary at 100 louis apiece, as he had
a great desire to do some riding. During his stay in Venice,
he said, he had been seized with a great longing to revisit
Vienna and Odessa ; but that would have to wait until the
following year. His more immediate plan was to go and
take the waters at Spa. At about this time, Colonel Stempowski was recalled to Russia, and as his promotion was
concerned, Richelieu raised no difficulty about his departure,
though he was as loth to see Stempkowski go as the Russian
was to part from him.

Even without Stempkowski, however, the duke could
scarcely be said to be alone, for it was during this period of
his travels about Europe that he became the victim of the
Queen of Sweden's unwelcome attentions, which were to
pursue him for the rest of his life. The wife of the former
Marshal Bernadotte, who had become King of Sweden, was
the daughter of a Marseilles merchant, another of whose
daughters had married Joseph Bonaparte. After one winter
in Sweden, she had announced that the climate of her
husband's new country did not suit her, and she returned to
Paris, where she took up her residence in the Rue d'Anjou.
Here, as Mme de Boigne informs us, " her servants and her

husband's ambassador addressed her as 'Your Majesty';
the rest of the world called her Mme Bernadotte." Towards
the end of Richelieu's ministry, she wrote and asked if she
could see him about some business concerning a relative.
In the days of the old régime it had been the custom for
ministers to call in person at the houses of great ladies who
had requests to make, and the duke continuing this tradition,
called upon the Queen of Sweden to inform her that her wishes
would be carried out. She then invited him to dinner, and
Richelieu, who as we have seen was fond of social life,
accepted her invitation. Let us now leave Mme de Boigne
to relate the sequel : " He did not suspect that he was thus
inspiring a madness which pursued him to the tomb. Mme
Bernadotte was seized with such a passion for the poor duke
that she followed him like a sleuth-hound throughout his
tour. At first he thought it extraordinary and could not
understand why she should always arrive three hours after
himself in every place where he stopped. Soon he began to
realise the fact that he was himself the attraction. Annoyance
overcame him. He concealed his route and his plans, laid
false scents, chose the gloomiest stopping-places and the
dirtiest inns. But it was wasted effort ; the accursed coach
invariably arrived three hours later than his own post-chaise.
It became a nightmare ! He realised, moreover, how much
this pursuit would lend itself to ridicule. He therefore
found a means of informing this royal heroine of the highroad
that he had decided to return to Paris at once if she persisted
in following him. On her side, she enquired of a doctor
whether the waters which the duke was to take were essential
for his health. On receiving an affirmative answer, she
decided to call a truce to her importunities and spent the
season at Geneva. However, as soon as it was ended, she
reopened the campaign." Arriving at the end of July in
Zurich, where he had intended to spend some days, Richelieu
was unnerved to find a bouquet waiting for him at the inn.
" Can it be that ' My Madwoman of a Queen ' has arrived ? "
he wrote to Rochechouart. If so, he would lose no time in

departing again, and he set off for Bâle on his way home. He remained in France for only a few weeks, however, in the course of which he paid visits to his wife at Courteilles and to his friend the Marquis de Vérac at Tremblay. After which, still determined not to be drawn back into the whirlpool of political life, he left France again at the beginning of September to go to Spa in order to take the waters ; which drew from Pozzo di Borgo the comment to Nesselrode that " M. de Richelieu is at Spa ; he has a horror of Paris, that is to say, of the place where he ought to be."

At Spa, the season was drawing to a close, few people were there, and those few were diminishing rapidly. This, however, suited Richelieu well enough, for without the distractions of social life he was able to take long rides on horseback for the good of his health. He wrote to Rochechouart that he was riding up to twenty miles every day, that he was living an absolutely solitary life, with—for the first time in his career—an abundance of books ready to hand. But alas, there was one blot on this otherwise peaceful scene : " ' My Madwoman of a Queen ' is here," he wrote to Léon de Rochechouart, " but in a severe incognito and so veiled that if I see her, I am never sure whether it is she, and so I go my way ; but it is all tiresome enough."

At the beginning of October, Richelieu left Spa and made a leisurely journey up the Rhine. The weather was very good and he was entranced with the pleasant aspect of the countryside where the grape harvest was in full swing. From there at the end of the month he went up to Holland. While he was staying in the Hague, a secret emissary arrived bearing a letter from Decazes, a note from Louis XVIII and the project of the proposed new electoral law of the double vote, over which the ministry, as usual, was finding itself in grave difficulties through the violent opposition of the Ultras. Richelieu was entreated once more to lend his name for the purpose of pulling the ministerial chestnuts out of the fire. But the duke still held firm to his resolve not to be trapped a second time. On the 13th November, he wrote to

Decazes that if he could have thought it to be of any use, he would have put himself at the King's disposal, but a careful examination of the situation had convinced him that he did not possess the necessary qualities to overcome the obstacles. He was, however, resolved to do everything he could to support the government in its generous enterprise, and it might be that in an indirect way he would be able to render far more useful service. Finding Richelieu immovable, the cabinet appealed to the King to exert his influence, but in view of the failure of his first appeal, Louis XVIII did not feel it consonant with his royal dignity to risk a second rebuff. Dessolles, Louis and St. Cyr thereupon resigned, and the cabinet was hastily cobbled together in time for the opening of the new session by replacing them with Pasquier, Roy and Latour-Maubourg, while Decazes became President of the Council.

At the beginning of December, Richelieu returned at last to Paris, driven back, alleges Mme de Boigne, by the renewed activity of his " Mad Queen." He thought it easier to defend himself on home territory, and the Master of the Hunt's house in the Place Vendôme was now ready for him, so that he was able to take up his residence there. But the " Mad Queen's " persecution of him seems only to have been intensified by his return to Paris. " She had rooms near those which he used," says Mme de Boigne, " and he could not appear at one window without seeing the Queen at another. As soon as he went out she was after him ; her carriage followed his. She stopped when he stopped, got out when he got out, waited for him whenever he paid a call. . . . If he went into a shop she followed him, waited until he had gone out, and then bought the object which he had chosen and sent him another copy. . . . M. de Richelieu required exercise, and often went to the garden of the Tuileries ; the Queen pursued him there also, but she observed that her presence drove him away, and she did not wish to deprive him of his walk. One day she arrived at Mme Recamier's house radiant with joy, and announced that she had arranged with her tailors to have a dress of different cut and colour for every day. M. de Richelieu would not then recognise her at a distance, and would not turn away his head until she had had the happiness of looking at him for a moment in the face. On one occasion when he was talking with animation, she had secured a bow by passing close at hand and making him a bow which he returned before he recognised her. She came in delight to relate this triumph to Mme Recamier, who made vain attempts to rouse a little natural dignity in the heart of the Queen of Sweden by reproaching her for continuing attentions thus constantly disregarded, seeing that the duke's refusal was becoming as violent as the energy of his pursuer, and indeed bordered upon the brutal. But she liked him in that mood, ' even when he was a little fierce.' " Nor were her husband's continued appeals to her to return any more successful ; she merely replied to his entreaties by sending doctors' certificates to the effect that the climate of Sweden was unsuited to her health.

So 1819 passed quietly into the first month of 1820, and though Spain blazed up into revolution, the month went by uneventfully in France. Across the Channel, the life of a poor old mad king shut up in Windsor Castle gently flickered out, and Louis XVIII designated Richelieu as his ambassador extraordinary to go over to England and present his compliments to the new king, his very good friend of the days of exile. The duke began to make his arrangements for the journey ; he was to leave for England on the 14th February. But an unbalanced fanatic by the name of Louvel had been brooding over the supposed wrongs of the French nation, and the sharp knife with which he thought to find a remedy was to set off a train of events which brought Richelieu's interlude of peace and freedom to an abrupt conclusion.

CHAPTER VIII

RECAPTURED

On the evening of Sunday the 13th February, the Duc de Berry, Monsieur's younger son, had gone with his wife to a special performance at the Opera. As he was handing her into the carriage to go home a man rushed at him, dealing him what he took to be a violent blow on the chest. But the blow was the impact of a knife being driven deeply into the duke's chest by Louvel. The unfortunate prince was carried into one of the administrative offices of the Opera House, where he expired some hours later. The child which his wife was expecting would now be the sole heir of the older branch of the Bourbons, since the Duc d'Angoulême, Monsieur's elder son, had no children.

The assassination of the Duc de Berry was like the sudden breaking of a dam behind which Royalist hatred of Decazes had been piling up; the torrent now poured forth with unrestrained violence. In the Chamber, the Ultra deputy, Clausel de Coussergues seriously proposed that Decazes should be arraigned as an accessory to the murder, though the saner Royalists disapproved of his proposal. But even the more moderate felt that Decazes through his flirtations with Liberalism had at least a moral responsibility for the crime. Nor could the unhappy Decazes rely upon the support of his colleagues in the cabinet. Even Pasquier had made no attempt to defend him in the Chamber at the time of Clausel de Coussergues' denunciation, which was only equalled by the violent attacks on Decazes in the Royalist Press. Indeed Mathieu de Montmorency warned him that his life was in danger. The King meanwhile was sruggling to preserve his favourite's position in face of violent opposition from his own family; on the 16th February, he had a particularly painful interview with them in the course of which both Monsieur and his niece, the Duchesse d'Angoulême threw themselves on their knees before him, imploring him to dismiss Decazes for the sake of the favourite himself, whose life, Madame assured the King, was in danger. Decazes saw the impossibility of his position and urged the King to call upon Richelieu. Louis still remembered the duke's previous refusals and was unwilling to approach him again personally; though he did not forbid Decazes to do so. With this encouragement, Decazes hastened to call upon Richelieu, showing him the royal letter as a form of authority.

But he found Richelieu as adamant as before. The duke stood by what he had written to Decazes from the Hague in November; he had nothing to add or withdraw from what he had written at that time. He did not believe that he was indispensable; others could do the task required, and do it better than he, who " had always been the *bête noire* of the Ultras." With prophetic insight he added to Decazes: " Monsieur promised you his support. That did not prevent him from withdrawing it from you, in the gravest circumstances and without motive. What he has just done against you he would do against me. There is nothing to guarantee the duration of the undertaking he declares himself ready to give if I accept power." Decazes reported his lack of success to the King. On the 18th, Monsieur paid another visit to his brother, pressing him once more to dismiss the favourite. This time Louis could struggle no further, and he agreed that he would sacrifice Decazes if Richelieu could be induced to take up the burden once more.

Monsieur, therefore, directed on to the duke the full volume of his entreaties, appealing at the same time to the Marquis de Vérac, now Governor of the château of Versailles, to use his influence with Richelieu. The much-harried duke had by that time taken to his bed with what Charles de Rémusat described as " the colic habitual to him on such occasions," but Monsieur's emissaries pursued him even to that refuge. First came Jules de Polignac, an envoy full of specious arguments; but he had no better success than Decazes. All day long throughout the 20th February, Monsieur continued to send message after message of entreaty. Finally he appeared in person at Richelieu's bedside. " One man less : Decazes ; one man more : you. That is all I want " ; said he ingratiatingly, " make up your ministry as seems best to you, and be sure that I shall approve everything, support everything. Your policy shall be mine and I will be your foremost soldier." But Richelieu, knowing Monsieur only too well, still held back. Then Monsieur solemnly vowed, on the dead body of his son and on the word of honour of "a prince to a gentleman", that he would support Richelieu. Upon receiving this undertaking, the duke yielded. But he had no illusions as to the size and difficulty of the task before him : " They want my death ! " he cried. " They will have it ! " Charles de Rémusat, who could always be relied upon to keep his mother informed of the latest tales going the round of the Paris *salons*, wrote to her that Monsieur had been to see Richelieu ; that the duke, remarking gruffly that he felt very ill, had turned his face to the wall and that Monsieur had then threatened to bring Madame (the Duchesse d'Angoulême) to see him ; at which bleak prospect the duke was said to have capitulated instantly.

To his old friend Sicard, however, Richelieu wrote : " You will have heard what Providence has decided to do with me, in spite of myself—but there are circumstances stronger than men. It is a question of combating the eternal enemies of social order ; it is a fight to the death." He obviously considered that the long struggle between royalism and revolution had now reached a critical point where all defenders of royalty must be mobilised, however unwilling they might be to enter the fray. But his heart was wrung at the thought of having to abandon all the plans he had made for the immediate future : " I need not tell you," he wrote again to Sicard, " what I have suffered, and still suffer, at having had to renounce the good fortune of finding myself once more among you. Only a year ago at this time, I was so happy and flattering myself that I was going to remain so for a long time to come. I was then at Leghorn, where you gave me such a pleasant reception. If I had set out for England, where I was to go in order to greet the new king, only two days sooner, I should have avoided this misery ; for my horses were harnessed to the calash in which I was to set forth, at the actual moment when I heard of the fatal happening of the Duc de Berry. You see on what hangs the destiny of men."

Richelieu was now faced once more with the task of forming a cabinet, which he drew largely from among moderate Royalists. The office of Minister of Police was revived, and the portfolio bestowed upon one of them, Baron Mounier, who had served in the Napoleonic adminis- tration. But true to his principle of trying to maintain contact with even the most extreme section of the Royalist party, Richelieu also admitted to his cabinet as ministers without portfolio the Ultra leader, Villèle, and his lieutenant, Corbière. Count Jean de Villèle, a former naval officer of the old régime, had started his career as deputy by represent- ing Toulouse in the *Chambre introuvable*. He survived the dissolution of that Chamber, and when the new house assembled was to be found once more in the front line of his considerably shrunken party. He soon became its leader. Yet with the cautious prudence which was one of his most outstanding characteristics, as the Ultras lost ground through their own violence, he himself became more moderate, and on entering Richelieu's cabinet he was at pains to emphasise that he was a mere beginner in politics who had much to learn.

Richelieu, though President of the Council in the new government, was this time a minister without portfolio. But his chief concern was with foreign affairs, since his knowledge of other European countries and courts, as well as his friend- ship with the Tsar, gave him special qualifications for acting in an advisory capacity to Pasquier, the actual Foreign

Minister.   He also gave a good deal of attention to army
business, working with one of the chiefs of division, General
Decaux, in an effort to supplement the work of the not very
brilliant War Minister, Latour-Maubourg.   In the Chamber,
Richelieu seldom addressed the House, since he was no
orator, and was not at his ease in the tribune.   Pasquier was
therefore the chief spokesman for the ministry ; coming as
he did from a distinguished legal family, he was a polished
and tactful speaker—even though his discretion was to earn
him the nickname of " the serpent " among Ultra firebrands.
Yet Pasquier's oratorical gifts were, in fact, a valuable asset
to the ministry, for as he himself tells us in his memoirs, the
parties in the Chamber at this period were so narrowly
balanced that every question raised could be a potential
source of danger to the life of the cabinet, if not well handled.
It only needed an imprudent word, a badly chosen argument,
the ill-timed expression of some hope or fear on one side or
the other, to cause a dozen floating votes which could decide
an issue to pass either to right or left as the case might be.
Thus the tribune could be the scene of success or reverse on
the most important issues.   Pasquier emphasises that it was not
eloquence that was needed but tactical skill.   For the ministers
realised that their primary aim must be to preserve their
majority, just as the opposition realised that with forces so
nearly equal, they must not neglect any opportunity of
scoring over the government.   This parity of forces, which
kept the unfortunate ministry on a perpetual tight-rope, was
the result of the system of annual renewals of one-fifth of the
Chamber, which had been maintained under the electoral law
of 1817, and which had each year brought such a steady
increase to the numbers of the Left that by 1820 they had
almost reached equality with the Right.   Obviously if such a
state of affairs were allowed to continue, it could not be long
before the Left would be in a majority ; hence Richelieu's
sincere belief in the necessity of altering the electoral law.
   But the proposal to restore power to the aristocratic landowners of the District Assemblies had roused such furious

opposition from all groups of the Left and from the Doctrinaires that the bill sponsored by the Comte de Serre, and finally
carried in June was the compromise of the " double vote," by
which members of the Collèges de Département could also
vote in the Collèges d'Arrondissement; while partial
renewals of the Chamber were only to start after it had been
sitting for five years. Like all compromises, the bill was
satisfying to neither side, and it was only carried after the
most violent scenes in the Chamber. Richelieu was horrified
at the spirit revealed in the speeches of deputies, and wrote to
de Serre : " You will have seen what a grievous scene of
scandal the presentation [of the electoral law] has occasioned.
Royer-Collard, a man whom I see with so much regret in the
ranks of the Opposition, has announced that since anarchy has
been introduced into the Chamber, each one must turn it to
his own credit. I was present at the sitting of the Chamber,
and I cannot tell you how upset I was with a spectacle whose
like has not been seen since the good old days of the Convention. Unhappy the nation which sees its dearest interests thus
treated by the men who are charged with them ! "

But, by the end of the session, Richelieu had had enough,
not only of Royer-Collard, but of all the Doctrinaires. They
were still members of the Council of State, but their constant
criticism and open opposition was a perpetual thorn in the
side of the ministry from the very moment of its taking office.
" These gentlemen," the duke wrote bitterly to de Serre,
" understand representative government according to their
own ideas, and not in the only way in which it can exist."
Moreover the Ultras, represented in the cabinet by Villèle
and Corbière, were sworn enemies of the Doctrinaires, whose
share in the downfall of the *Chambre introuvable* and their long
support of Decazes were neither forgotten nor forgiven. As
soon as the parliamentary session came to an end, therefore,
Richelieu lost no time in having them removed from the
Council of State. Guizot was the first to go. He was closely
linked with the professors and students who were in the
vanguard of Left agitation, and in Pasquier's view, had

behaved most improperly in the Chamber by descending from
the special tribune reserved for Councillors of State, and taking
an impassioned part in the debates. Guizot's dismissal was
rapidly followed by that of Camille Jordan, whose violent
opposition to the repressive measures which followed the
murder of the Duc de Berry marked him in the eyes of his
colleagues as the apologist and defender of sedition. Royer-
Collard's fate caused some agonies of indecision both to
Richelieu and to de Serre. He was probably the most brilliant
of all the Doctrinaires ; he was also an orator of outstanding
rhetorical power, in the grand (and rather ponderous) style
dear to members of the old Constituent Assembly. But
although not without a certain grave dignity, he was pedantic,
overbearing in manner, and of a quite limitless self-suffi-
ciency. He had quarrelled bitterly with de Serre over the
electoral law, although they had been life-long friends, and
Richelieu found him more than trying. His persistent opposition to every item of the budget, so often appearing inspired
by party feeling rather than by genuine constitutional scruples,
finally overcame the hesitation of both Richelieu and de Serre,
and Royer-Collard was also removed from the Council. The
unfortunate result, however, was that the enraged Doctrinaires now moved over definitely to the ranks of the Left.
With their extinction as a separate party, the whole galaxy of
political groups completed the process of fusing into two
simple divisions of Right and Left, and the domestic political
issue became narrowed down into a struggle for power
between the two.

CHAPTER IX

EUROPE IN TURMOIL

It was not only in France that the seeds of Liberalism were germinating with results so disturbing to the generation which had lived through the French Revolution and which continued to classify protagonists of the new ideas under the old name of " Jacobins." The ferment of unrest which in Germany had been met in the previous year 1819 with the Carlsbad Decrees, was to erupt into full violence within the first few months of the year in which Richelieu took office for the second time. In Spain, exasperated by the absolutist reaction following the restoration of Ferdinand VII, who, like his cousins in Paris, had forgotten nothing and learnt nothing, liberal elements in the Spanish army had already celebrated the dawn of the new year by a revolt in which they demanded the acceptance by the King of the constitution originally proposed by the Cortes of Cadiz in 1812. But as the session of the French Chambers drew to a close in the summer of 1820, an even more serious complication was added to the tangled skein of European affairs. Naples, though under the easygoing rule of an old and popular King—known affectionately to his subjects as Nasone, owing to the imposing dimensions of the royal nose—yet felt herself obliged, under the combustible influence of the *Carbonari*, to follow the fashion and demand a constitution, also to be based on that of Cadiz. Revolution in Naples, however, raised far more complicated issues than the outbreak in Spain, with the possibility of the contagion spreading northwards to those parts of Italy under Austrian control ; it had already reached the Papal States. Austria was losing no time in bestirring herself and in assembling troops on the banks of the Po, with the obvious intention, if need be, of quenching the fire in the south by force of arms.

Richelieu had always insisted on France's need of a period of rest and recovery, sparing no pains to impress upon her ambassadors his view of the policy which her condition imposed upon her. The representatives of France everywhere, he declared, must work to overcome the mistrust inspired by her past history ; her aim henceforth must be internal recovery and the rebirth of her commerce and industry. In European affairs, though he made no secret of his inclination towards Russia, whose Tsar he considered to have saved France from dismemberment in 1815, he held, nevertheless, that France must adopt an attitude of neutral detachment, above all until she could be more certain of the future alignment of Europe. No action must be taken by her which might appear to be a departure from that principle ; though Richelieu did not view with disfavour the idea of setting up Bourbon monarchies in South America. But the Royalists, even some members of the cabinet, felt that it was essential for the restored Bourbon monarchy in France to score some resounding success in European affairs, if only to offset the victories of the Empire. The French, said Chateaubriand, would forget liberty if one could give them glory ; victories rather than charters were what were needed to reconcile them with royalty. The Left were just as eager for action by France, though they saw her in a different rôle : they considered that France, as befitted a modern constitutional monarchy, should come forth as the champion of Liberalism against reaction, placing herself at the head of the Liberal movements which were seething in Europe.

The Neapolitan outbreak therefore placed Richelieu's ministry in a peculiarly difficult position. Apart from the eagerness of both political parties for some form of foreign adventure, the head of the House of Bourbon could scarcely remain a passive spectator while Austria, the centuries-old rival of France in Italy, proceeded to march in and regulate the internal affairs of a kingdom ruled by a Bourbon prince,

T.S.—13

even if a distinctly odd one. Yet for France to advocate armed intervention in the cause of counter-revolution would undoubtedly arouse the most furious hostility in the ranks of the Left. They were already causing the government enough trouble with the plot hatched under cover of meetings in the emporium known as the *Bazar français*, a plot which was merely to be one of many more during the course of the succeeding two years. It was clear, however, that some action must be taken by France, and a memorandum was therefore sent from Louis XVIII to the Allied Courts suggesting a conference on the lines of that held two years before in Aix-la-Chapelle. But this time it did not meet with the hoped-for response ; only the Tsar was willing for the kind of meeting it envisaged. Decazes, whose controversial presence had been removed from France by his being made ambassador in London, was harping on the need for keeping in step with England, who was maintaining an attitude of aloof neutrality.

Yet France could not afford to offend Russia, her only friend and a possible ally ; at the same time the Tsar, on his side, was determined not to have his plans upset by unilateral action on the part of France. His views were conveyed to Richelieu : recent events in France culminating in the murder of the Duc de Berry, had left him, he said, completely unable to feel any confidence in her stability. Even though Richelieu had now returned to be at the head of the government, it was to be impressed on the duke that there could be no change in Russian policy simply on that account. The old relations which had existed between Pozzo di Borgo and Richelieu during the years of the occupation were not to be renewed ; Pozzo was henceforth to preserve a certain detachment from affairs, and contact between the two would be in secret and unofficial, Pozzo's reports being sent as private letters, no longer as official documents. Though the Tsar's affection for Richelieu remained unaltered and he would continue to send his observations through Pozzo, they would in future be to Richelieu as a person, not as a minister. Alexander announced firmly that no partial action on the part of France would serve any useful purpose ; the primary interest of the Powers was to make common cause against the common enemy. France, he concluded, must first of all put her own house in order ; if she mediated, it would be at the joint request of the Powers and not on her own initiative. The Tsar therefore addressed a formal proposal to all the allied Courts, inviting them to send plenipotentiaries to some town in Silesia where he could meet the Emperor of Austria and the King of Prussia, and where French and English delegates would be able to arrive by the time he had finished his own affairs in Warsaw. The little town of Troppau was finally chosen for the purpose. Metternich would of course have much preferred Vienna, but the Tsar was not going to give Austria the advantage of having the congress in her own capital.

Although the idea of having the Congress had been originally put forward by Louis XVIII, Decazes was now working upon the King from London. He pointed out that Castlereagh had refused to attend the Congress ; if Richelieu went, in order to please the Ultras and Russia, then constitutional France would be leaving to England the honour and profit of setting up in the eyes of Europe as the one truly Liberal kingdom. Was this to the real interest of the Bourbons ? The King took fright. So also, but for a different reason, did the Tsar : if the influence of Decazes could still be so potently exercised upon the King even from the other side of the Channel, what might not happen if Richelieu left Paris to go as far away as Troppau ? The Tsar hastened to convey his anxiety to the duke through his minister Capodistrias ; everyone knew what had been the unfortunate results of Richelieu's absence at Aix-la-Chapelle in 1818. Nor had the duke forgotten the events of that year. He decided not to go to Troppau ; France like England would send only ambassadors. But the problem of choosing these was not easy. The Tsar expressed the hope that Caraman, the French ambassador in Vienna, would not be

among them, since he was known to be under the thumb of
Metternich.   But in September, Richelieu wrote to Capodistrias : " To banish Caraman on this occasion would have
been to show towards Prince Metternich a mistrust of which
already he is only too prone to accuse us ; but we thought
it would please you to associate La Ferronays with him
[Caraman]. . . . In a few days we shall send him his instructions, and the one he will have the greatest pleasure in carrying
out will surely be that of drawing close to you, to whom he
cannot do better than join himself in language and opinions."
The Tsar had already intimated his approval of La Ferronays,
the ambassador in St. Petersburg, as a possible choice ; but
La Ferronays was appalled to find that Richelieu was not
going to the Congress.   The duke's non-appearance, he pro-
tested, would be most unfortunate, as it was France who had
particularly asked for the meeting, and the Tsar had made a
point of acceding promptly, while rebutting Metternich's
attempts to draw him into discussions on Italy without the
presence of the other allied representatives.   If La Ferronays
went to Troppau, it must be on the absolute understanding
that Caraman was to be head of the delegation, and La
Ferronays merely his adjutant ; France could not speak with
two voices.

    But Richelieu and Pasquier had other ideas about the part
to be played by their two representatives.   Since Caraman was
the tool of Metternich, La Ferronays was to be France's real
envoy, and he was to sound the Tsar privately about the
possibility of a closer bond between France and Russia, with
a view to joint mediation between Naples and Austria.   La
Ferronays would be able to checkmate both Metternich and
Caraman because he would approve nothing which did not
have the consent of the Five Courts ; this would be a perfectly safe procedure, because it was certain that England
would always refuse to be drawn in to anything.   Caraman's
mission was thus merely fictitious, to preserve appearances
with Metternich, and he must on no account be allowed to
know anything of the task assigned to La Ferronays.

The unfortunate result of this policy, however, was that when the proceedings opened at Troppau on the 23rd October with Metternich's note in which he demanded a mandate for Austrian intervention in Naples, the two members of the French delegation provided a painful spectacle of disunity. La Ferronays declared outright that Austria was laying down principles which would make it impossible for constitutional governments to act with other members of the Alliance; while Caraman hastened to inform both Metternich and the British ambassador from Vienna that La Ferronays was only expressing a private opinion which was not shared either by his colleague or his government! La Ferronays wrote plaintively to Pasquier that there should be someone to speak with authority for France, that only Richelieu could have done this, and that Metternich was saying that there were two Frances at Troppau. By the 20th November, the Austrian, Prussian and Russians cabinets had taken to conducting their meetings in closed session, merely notifying the French and English delegates of their decisions when these had been already arrived at. The Congress finally broke up without having reached any concrete decisions, other than the publication of the Troppau Circular with its alarming declaration of the right of the absolute monarchies to intervene in their neighbours' internal affairs, and the decision to continue the discussions at Laibach the following January in a further congress to which the King of Naples was to be invited.

At Laibach, the French delegation was enlarged by the addition of Blacas, then ambassador in Rome, who arrived with the King of Naples. He was the bearer of a secret letter from Louis XVIII, only to be produced in case of necessity, to the effect that if the views of the French delegates differed, he was to have over-riding authority. But this did nothing to clarify French policy in the meantime. Richelieu, hoping to find a middle path through the thorny thickets of intervention, had instructed Caraman to support non-intervention up to a point, as far as could be done without clashing with the Tsar's ideas; but the delegates were on no account to subscribe to anything which could entail a declaration of war against Naples. Representatives from other Italian states had been invited to attend at Laibach, and Richelieu appears to have hoped that they would support France in a more definite and active policy. But at a distance of several hundred miles from the scene of the Congress, the duke was hopelessly handicapped when dealing with an opponent as adroit as Metternich. When the Italian delegates arrived, having been kept out of all meetings of the congress up to the 26th January, they were then invited to sign the minutes of the first conferences which had been drawn up so as to inform them only about such matters as Metternich considered it desirable for them to know. Since the Italian princes were much more frightened of revolution than they were even of allying with Metternich, their delegates obediently attached their signatures to the documents, and the ground was neatly cut from under the feet of the French representatives. Without Italian support, yet not wishing to part from the Italian states, they resigned themselves to being carried along in the stream whose course was being directed by the Austrian Chancellor. Richelieu's despatch specifically instructing them not to support any declaration of war against Naples had apparently not yet reached them, and Blacas, considering that the moment had now come for the production of his secret letter, declared to his colleagues his determination to adhere to the resolutions of the Congress rather than leave Naples in the grip of revolution. Moreover, he pointed out, France must not break with Russia and risk being cast out of the European concert.

When Richelieu learnt that his despatch had arrived too late, he would not avail himself of the clause by which the French representatives specifically reserved liberty of action to their government. Although La Ferronays did in fact urge the cabinet to disavow the action of the delegates, Richelieu limited himself to a request that they should notify the Congress that they had gone beyond their instructions. He did, however, send a note to be presented or read to the

Powers at Laibach in which it was stated that France could not subscribe to the general right of intervention postulated in the Troppau Circular, and certainly not to its application in the affairs of Naples. Nor could France, pursued Richelieu, base her conduct on a principle she did not admit; but she would seek as a neutral to do everything possible to soften the rigours and abridge the term of armed intervention.

Meanwhile the Tsar, through Pozzo di Borgo, had been impressing on Richelieu that France was obviously the Power to deal with the revolution in Spain, as Austria was about to do in Naples. This argument greatly embarrassed both Richelieu and Pasquier, neither of whom had any desire to see France embroiled in such a dangerous adventure. Pasquier was not averse to an enterprising foreign policy, but he felt that a break with Spain at that moment would be merely playing into the hands of the Left, who desired nothing better than a Franco-Spanish rupture as the means of achieving the triumph of Liberalism in both countries. To Pozzo di Borgo, Richelieu wrote while sitting in a session of the Chamber of Peers, which " is not a good place to deal with such grave matters as those you raise, but it is the only moment I have available in the extraordinary life I am leading. Six hours in this Chamber and three or four each day in councils or committees; there goes the greater part of the day, filled up without having the time to read or write a letter." Referring to the Tsar's promptings on the subject of Spain, Richelieu continued : " I cannot consider this overture without the greatest uneasiness. I am convinced that such an attempt would have for the House of Bourbon the same results as had the war in Spain for Buonaparte."

In March, the European situation was further complicated by two fresh outbreaks of what the British Foreign Secretary solemnly described as " the organised spirit of insurrection which is systematically propagating itself throughout Europe." This time the storm centres were Piedmont and Moldavia. France did not relish the prospect of Austrian troops entering Piedmont any more than she did in the case of Naples ; but there was nothing she could do to prevent it. Richelieu tentatively proposed to England a joint mediation, but the attitude of the British cabinet was not encouraging : they did not feel that mediation would be a feasible policy unless a joint appeal were to be made by both the contending parties. Richelieu himself was emphatic that France, placed as she was, could not and must not take any direct part in military operations prepared by the northern Powers. Any such action, he maintained, would be impossible for her, both from the state of her army and finances, and from the distrust which any active interference by her in Italian affairs would arouse among the other Powers.

Meanwhile, in the Chamber, the Austrian march on Naples was causing scenes of fevered excitement. The Left, carried away by wishful thinking and the memories of their own early struggles in the days of the Revolution, predicted the most fantastic successes for the revolutionaries in Italy, and the rout of the Austrian army. " The Austrians have entered the Abruzzi ; they will not come out again ! " cried General Foy in the Chamber, to the accompaniment of frenzied applause from the benches of the Left. But when the news came that the Austrians had actually entered Naples without striking a blow, in the Liberal ranks there was consternation, which became even greater when a month later the revolution in Piedmont was extinguished on the field of Novara. It was now the turn of the Royalists to exult, and they hailed the outcome of Italian affairs with rapture as the triumph of legitimacy over revolution ; while Richelieu wrote to Pozzo di Borgo : " Who the devil could have expected that after so much bluster and bragging, the Neapolitans should have been yet more Neapolitan than they have ever been ? " But both parties in the Chamber were smarting at the frustration of French policy in Italy. The Ultras felt that France had been denied the opportunity of taking action there for the recovery of her old influence ; the Left saw not only a blow to national prestige, but a lamentable failure on the part of the government to support the Liberal cause.

Yet there were still possibilities in the Balkans, for although the actual Moldavian rising soon collapsed, it lit a torch of insurrection in Greece which was to burn for nearly ten years, and by April the revolt had spread to the Morea. In the cabinet, Pasquier at first considered the Greek question with cautious prudence : only Russia, he maintained, stood to profit from it ; France would merely lose certain advantages, such as commercial privileges, without achieving any comparable gain. Her interest, therefore, obviously lay in maintenance of the *status quo*. But needless to say, this cautious attitude did not suit the firebrands of either Right or Left, and by October even Richelieu was beginning to feel that the old system of alliance with Turkey was a mistake now that the former European balance of Turkey and Sweden had been replaced by that of Prussia and Russia. In fact, by this time Richelieu and Pasquier had begun to sound Russia through La Ferronays about a possible partition of the Ottoman Empire in the event of its collapse—though Richelieu himself thought that this eventuality would be a misfortune, especially for Russia. The Tsar, however, had responded most cordially, inviting France to open a compass from Gibraltar to the Dardanelles, to pick within its range what she liked, and to count always on the friendly support of Russia, who he declared would be a far more certain and useful friend than the Porte, with whom France had been at such pains to try and recover her old influence and friendship. But both Richelieu and La Ferronays knew the Tsar and his unpredictable character well enough to receive Alexander's approaches with the greatest caution. France, declared Richelieu firmly, could do nothing without a definite resolution of support, in writing, from the Russian cabinet. Lainé, no longer a cabinet minister but still a member of the Council, viewed the Tsar's enthusiastic proposals with even greater circumspection. What was the use, said he, of inviting France to open a compass in the Mediterranean when England was in possession of all the strong points there ? France could only follow such a course by declaring herself on the side of Russia, thus alienating England. France's best policy, he maintained, was one of strict neutrality, however irksome to French dignity and pride ; indeed, any other policy was impossible for her without a sufficiently strong army and navy. This was a point which Richelieu well understood : France must have a strong naval force in the Levant, so that she would be ready to play her part in any coming events in that part of Europe, and she must have the means to pay for proper armaments. These could be raised, as in England, by public loan, for which twelve millions of *rentes* would be required. Pasquier drew up a memoir which was approved by the King, in which he advocated the assembling of a corps of 20,000–25,000 men in a central position ready for instant transfer where needed. This would, of course, entail the provision of a sufficiently strong naval force for their transport.

Frenchmen of both political parties acclaimed the prospect of action in alliance with Russia. But the Tsar began to realise that if he were to go to war against Turkey, he would be able to count only upon the support of France against the opposition of all his former allies. He recoiled. In vain Richelieu, seeing the perilous waters into which his ministerial barque was being carried on the tide of public opinion, besought the Tsar to act. The French nation, said the duke, was tired of inaction, and governments were never so near their fall as when they were despised by those who owed them obedience. Events were to show that Richelieu's forebodings were only too well founded.

CHAPTER X

FINAL DEFEAT

THE crushing of the revolutions in Naples and Piedmont had greatly raised the stock of the Royalists, while at the same time the prestige of the Left was falling as a result of the conspiracies which, beginning in 1820, were to continue sporadically during the following year. The damage done to the Liberal cause was reflected in the parliamentary elections, where the threatened Left majority began to recede both in 1820 and even more in 1821, when in the autumn of that year only ten Liberals were returned in elections held for eighty-seven seats.

But the triumph of their party over the Left only made the Ultras more aggressive and more impatient with the moderate Royalists whom Richelieu had gathered round him in his cabinet. One of the most rampant Ultras wrote to another, Hyde de Neuville, in April 1821, that Villèle and Corbière both agreed that it would be to their eternal shame and to the just discontent of the party which relied on them, if a more Royalist ministry could not be constituted before the end of the session ; that Villèle and Corbière felt this so strongly that they had decided to retire from the cabinet if their minimum demands were not met ; these being the portfolio of the Interior for Villèle and that of Public Education for Corbière. The latter was also continually agitating for the removal of eight or ten prefects, for no better reason than to be able " to do something for the Royalists." Richelieu replied, however, that all the prefects had been doing excellent work under difficult circumstances during the previous eighteen months, and he could not dream of sacrificing any. If one of them were to be found lacking and had to be relieved of his post, Richelieu said that he would certainly give the vacant place to one of the Royalists who, according to Corbière, were in need ; but he would never, he declared, sacrifice anyone unjustly.

In addition to the pressure thus being exercised by the two Ultra leaders in the cabinet, Richelieu was also suffering once more from Monsieur's intrigues. It was not, of course, to be expected that Monsieur, who in the words of his elder brother had " conspired against Louis XVI, conspires against me and will one day conspire against himself," could abandon his old ways all in a moment, even when he had given Richelieu his most solemn pledge of support. Monsieur was now constantly pressing the duke to get rid of Siméon, the Minister of the Interior, Mounier the Minister of Police, and Anglès the Police Prefect, since with the administration and police under Ultra control he calculated that he would be master of the kingdom. He was continually agitating also for compensation to be made to those of his followers who had lost all their property through emigration. At the same time he was particularly irritated at Richelieu's refusal to allow a number of Napoleonic generals to be placed on the retired list : " You will neither, then, take any measures against the ill disposed, nor do anything for the good ? " It was in vain that Richelieu replied that he had always had, and still had, the *émigrés* well in mind, but that nothing could be done until France's finances were in a more favourable situation ; it was, he said, an affair which would have to be handled with prudence, kept within wise limits, and above all, done at the most suitable moment. With regard to Anglès and Mounier, Richelieu unburdened himself on the subject to Capodistrias : " These two men, who abandoned everything in 1815 to follow the King to Ghent, should certainly be above suspicion, and as for their abilities, I doubt whether those whom it is proposed to put in their place would have any greater ; but they are party men, and the campaign being waged against Anglès and Mounier has no other aim than to put in their place two men devoted to M. de Talleyrand, whose intrigues continue in a state of constant activity. You can guess, after that, whether I would ever consent to such arrangements." Pasquier, whose sensible moderation made him intensely disliked by the Ultras, also became a target for their sniping tactics : would not Richelieu, they enquired ingratiatingly, take over the portfolio of Foreign Affairs again?

As for Villèle, he continued to angle for the portfolio of the Interior, which would enable him to retain his hold in the Chamber, but Richelieu was equally determined that he was not going to have it. Yet the duke was unwilling to break his link with the Ultras through the departure of Villèle and Corbière from the cabinet, and various combinations were suggested to keep the team together. Villèle was offered the portfolio of War, then that of the Marine, particularly suitable for a former naval officer, while Corbière was to have Public Education. Villèle then demanded the portfolio of War for Bellune. Even this, Richelieu was preparing to consider, but at this point Villèle fell under the baleful influence of Monsieur again. He suddenly veered round, declared to Richelieu that all the proposed arrangements were useless, and departed, in company with Corbière, back to Toulouse. Nevertheless, before leaving for the south, Villèle visited Richelieu privately and after expressing regret for his departure, he added : " Keep me my place ; I will find some way of taking it up again sooner or later ; . . . above all, do not let yourself be persuaded to dissolve the Chamber ; believe me, no one could give you more fatal advice. Such an act would make an irreparable break with the Royalists whom I and my friends will, if you do not go to that extremity, find some means of bringing back to you." Villèle's conduct throughout this period showed strange oscillations which give an appearance of duplicity, but which seem in actual fact to have been a conflict between the orders of Monsieur on the one hand, and his own prudent common sense on the other. But the trouble with Villèle was that he could not control the team of unmanageable horses he was trying to drive.

The immediate result of the departure of Villèle and

Corbière was unfortunately to deprive the cabinet of any support from the extreme Right and to leave them sandwiched between the intrigues of Decazes, who was still trying to edge his way back into power, and those of Monsieur and his set. Attacks on the ministry continued therefore, with unabated violence, the Court faction not even hesitating to inspire the scurrilous personal attack made in 1821 on Richelieu by General Donnadieu who accused him of corrupt practices. The harassed Richelieu, finding himself surrounded by the all too familiar network of hostility and intrigue, began to consider once more the possibility of retirement, and in his agonies of mind over the best course to pursue, worked himself up into his customary state of sickness and nervous prostration. Lainé, however, by pointing out the power still exercised over the King by Decazes, and the latter's manœuvres both in England and with Talleyrand, persuaded the duke to remain in office, at any rate for the time being.

In July, when the stormy and unusually long parliamentary session had at last come to an end, Richelieu turned his attention to a more rewarding field : public works. From the days of his first ministry, he had had in his mind a scheme for a network of canals to cover all France and provide her with a system of internal navigation to supplement her inadequate road communications. Napoleon had done much in the construction of highways for military purposes, but by the beginning of the Restoration these had fallen into disrepair, and although France was well endowed with large rivers, most of them had disadvantages from the navigational point of view. In the construction of canals, Richelieu planned to obtain the co-operation of capitalists by granting them not only interest on the money provided but certain advantages in connection with the canals themselves. In spite of encountering a good deal of obstructive opposition, he had the satisfaction of getting the necessary legislation passed for the construction and finishing of several of these canals, thus laying solid foundations for the ultimate fulfilment of his scheme.

Nor, in the midst of all his other preoccupations, had

Richelieu forgotten the affairs of New-Russia. His old friend the Abbé Nicolle had now returned to France, driven at last from Odessa in the previous year as a result of the hostile feeling which, since the French invasion, had developed in Russia against the employment of foreigners and of Jesuits in particular; however, in February 1821, the King had nominated him Rector of the Académie de Paris in the Sorbonne. In May, Richelieu was writing to another old friend, Charles Sicard, of his distress at a protectionist law which had just gone through the Chamber by 284 votes to 56, and which, he declared, was going to make an end of all commerce with Odessa, in addition to hitting Marseilles and Provence very badly. But " I had to keep absolute silence," he wrote, " for there would have been no hesitation in attributing my opinion to affection for that district, to the detriment of France. But there lies completely shattered my dream of linking France and Russia by the Black Sea. The interests of landowners, of whom our Chambers are largely composed, have carried the day against the consumers. In this affair there was neither Right nor Left ; the members most divided on political questions voted together in this one." For, while the Royalist landowners were eager to increase the income derived from the product of their lands, the industrials forming a large proportion of the Left were equally anxious for higher profits on their manufactures ; thus both parties were united in favouring a high tariff system. Since the period of great scarcity during which Richelieu had initiated the importation of Russian wheat, the good harvest of 1818, plus a general economic crisis had unfortunately caused a disastrous fall in the price of grain, and many wheat growers in France had been ruined. The enemies of the ministry were not slow in attributing this state of affairs to the duke's policy, and in the address to the King at the opening of the new parliamentary session on 5th November, Richelieu was accused of favouring Russian agriculture at the expense of France by causing the markets of the Midi to be flooded by grain from Odessa.

The extreme section of the Right had, in fact, lost none of their determination to pull down the ministry, and finding that Villèle's prudent caution would not serve their purpose, the most rabid Ultras had made overtures to their sworn enemies of the Left. The result of this unholy coalition was not only the direct attack on Richelieu but the venomous paragraph in the address to the King, in which the monarch was congratulated on his amicable relations with foreign Powers " in the just confidence that a peace so precious is not bought by sacrifices incompatible with the honour of the nation and the dignity of the crown." Louis XVIII replied with dignity to what was in effect an insult to himself through his ministers : in exile and in persecution, he said, he had upheld his rights and the honour of his own name as well as that of France. Seated upon the throne surrounded by his people, he was filled with indignation at the very idea that he could ever be thought to sacrifice the honour of the nation and the dignity of the crown. " I should like to think," concluded the old King, " that most of those who have voted this address have not fully weighed all the expressions in it." But the address was carried by a large majority against the ministry, and the agitated members of the cabinet thought to save it from destruction by sacrificing Pasquier, since he was known to be a particular target of Ultra enmity. They therefore besought Pasquier to resign ; but when Richelieu heard of it, and of Pasquier's intention of complying with his colleagues' wishes, he was much upset and accused Pasquier of leaving him in the lurch at a critical moment. He declared that if Pasquier persisted in resigning, he himself would instantly do the same. Unfortunately by this time Louis XVIII's health was rapidly failing ; indeed Richelieu confided to Villèle that it was of little use trying to discuss anything with the King, since he continually fell asleep during audiences—though Sosthènes de la Rochefoucauld asserted maliciously that this action was by no means so involuntary as it appeared. But there can be little doubt that Louis was becoming increasingly dominated by his brother, and by the

Ultras' tool, Mme du Cayla, whom they had inserted into the royal favour to take the place of Decazes. Thus, when Richelieu did succeed in presenting the difficulties of the situation to the King, the latter not only refused to dissolve the Chamber, but referred pointedly to the practice of British ministers of resigning when they could no longer command a majority in the house. Obviously Mme du Cayla had done her work only too well ; Richelieu could hope for no further support from that quarter. There seemed then only one more possible resort : a personal appeal to Monsieur, the true source of the ministry's difficulties.

On the following morning, therefore, Richelieu asked for an audience with the heir to the throne, with whom he had a long discussion, explaining the situation as best he could " whenever Monsieur left time ; for he has the habit of hardly ever letting one reply, which is a sure method of always being right." Monsieur proposed that Richelieu should dispense with the existing members of the cabinet, save only de Serre and Roy, and that he should receive back into it Villèle and Corbière as Ministers of Finance and the Interior respectively. But Richelieu maintained that he could not possibly sacrifice the colleagues who had been through so many struggles with him, and he appealed to Monsieur to put an end to the Ultra manœuvres which had been making the Chamber a battlefield. Monsieur, however, responded blandly that Richelieu was mistaken in supposing that he had any power of that kind over his followers, and that, in any case, he made it a rule now never to interfere in such matters. Richelieu retorted : " I am speaking too seriously for Monsieur to believe that I should accept such an answer. I am asking him to keep his plighted word. Monsieur cannot have forgotten that in the first moments after the death of his son, he made use of the most pressing entreaties to induce me, in the midst of that horrible crisis, to take up again the direction of affairs. I only yielded upon his solemnly pledged word that he and all his followers would support me to the utmost of their power. . . . Monseigneur, it is this

word of a prince given to a gentleman that I now invoke."
Monsieur's reply was given with the same airy nonchalance
as before: "Ah, my dear duke, you took the words too
literally. And anyway, circumstances were then so difficult!"
Richelieu, speechless at this final revelation of the character
of his future King, looked fixedly at the prince, then, in
defiance of all etiquette, abruptly turned his back and without
uttering another word, strode from the room, slamming the
door violently behind him. He went straight to Pasquier,
who relates that he was horrified at the duke's pallor and
agitation on entering. "I am overwhelmed," said Richelieu,
"I can hardly look you in the face, so ashamed am I of the
man whose words I am going to repeat to you." He then
gave an account of his conversation with Monsieur; after
which painful recital, he concluded by saying: "You see
what remains for us to do. It is impossible to work with
this Chamber; the majority which has declared itself against
us has Monsieur for its chief. It might still be possible to
get the King to sign the ordinance for a dissolution; one
might address oneself to the country and so obtain the justice
we cannot get from the political groups. But, in that case,
who would suffer? The King's brother, the heir to the
throne, who, owing to the precarious health of the old King,
may soon be summoned to take up his heritage. You yourself
said to me three months ago, M. Pasquier, that we cannot
compromise him, we cannot undermine his authority. For
the last two years we have done everything we could to
develop, to strengthen monarchic feeling; it is not for us
to undo this work. . . . Let us then leave the power to
those who covet it with such longing. We retire, leaving
the party of the Revolution powerless and disarmed, France
calm and prosperous, the army re-organised, finance re-estab-
lished, with a credit which has never been better. The future
will render us justice, and our consciences will let us enjoy a
well-deserved rest after our years of labour." Pasquier agreed
with Richelieu that retirement was the only possible course
left to them. Their colleagues proved to be of the same

opinion ; so on the morning of the following day, 12th
December, Richelieu carried the resignation of his ministry
to the King, who received the news with a placid calm
remarkably different from his attitude in 1818. Under the
circumstances, he observed, Richelieu could not have followed
any other course.

It was customary for the outgoing minister to advise the
King on the choice of a new cabinet, but as the duke at the
conclusion of his wearing ordeal had promptly taken to his
bed, the duty fell to Pasquier of presenting the list of suggested new ministers to the King, who declared that his
brother would first have to see it. Two days of negotiation
then followed before it was possible to arrive at the selection
of a cabinet equally satisfactory to Monsieur and to his
henchmen Villèle and Corbière, not to mention Mme du
Cayla. Meanwhile, Talleyrand had not been wasting his
time : the very day of Richelieu's resignation, he had hastened
to pay a personal call on the duke, for which he duly received
Richelieu's polite thanks—and nothing more. Fearing,
therefore, that the true purpose of his visit had not been
understood, Talleyrand uncovered it a month later by sending
his brother Archambaud to the duke with the formal proposal of an alliance. Richelieu did not trouble to make any
reply to this proposition, which in truth he considered merely
as a bad joke.

But though Richelieu may have spoken to Pasquier of
their exit from office with a certain philosophical detachment,
when writing to his old friend Sicard he did not attempt to
conceal his pain at the overthrow of his ministry just at a
time, he said, when it had brought the country to a state of
well-being it had not known for forty years. " I have great
regrets on the subject," he wrote, " and this time my liberty
does not give me any pleasure. We were on the road to
prosperity, there was much to do, and it was pleasant and
flattering to attach one's name to it. But now I begin to be
resigned and to taste the sweets of independence. You will
appreciate that in this position my thoughts turn naturally

towards Odessa. I am planning to come and see you next summer ; I cannot come any sooner because there are those who would not fail to say that I was going to sell French secrets to Russia, just as they accuse me of selling her interests. For you must know that while at your end we are accused of being too English, here I have been accused by those hostile to me, of betraying France for the benefit of Russia. I must therefore remain a few months in Paris, before contemplating any travels ; but towards the spring, I plan to put myself on the road to Vienna, and from there reach the shores of the Black Sea."

CHAPTER XI

JOURNEY'S END

Since Richelieu felt obliged to remain within reach of Paris for some little while to come, he began to pay longer and more frequent visits to Courteilles than he had ever done up to that time. Now that he and his wife were both in their fifties, circumstances were drawing them closer together, and Richelieu's appreciation of her character was gradually overcoming even the disability of her physical appearance. The utter peacefulness of Courteilles, the gentle wit and understanding kindliness of his wife, her mother and their circle of friends, whose conversation was of literature and philosophy never of politics, must have been a refuge indeed to the tired, disheartened and ailing man, after the bitter-tongued strife of Paris and the ingratitude of the Bourbons whose cause he had served to the last ounce of his strength.

There is probably a good deal of truth in Mme de Boigne's assertion that the Bourbons never forgave Richelieu for his repeated refusals to follow in the steps of his grandfather by taking up a post in the King's household which would have condemned him to lead the sterile life of a courtier. But what is still more sure is that Monsieur never forgave him for his refusal to lend the prestige of his name to Ultra intrigue by presiding as an imposing figure-head over a cabinet of Monsieur's followers. Further fuel was added to the resentment of the heir apparent—which according to the prevailing wind meant that of the entire royal family as well—by the fact that the stringent Press law proposals which ushered in the new Ultra ministry of Villèle had been opposed in the Upper House by certain members of the last cabinet. From this time onward, the unfortunate Richelieu, who by virtue of his nominal post of Master of the Royal Hunt was still obliged to appear occasionally for lunch at the Tuileries, was treated by the whole royal family not merely with coldness, but at times with deliberate spite. On a certain occasion, for instance, when the Duchesse d'Angoulême had had some cream sent to her from a little domain which she had recently acquired, she took great pains to offer some of it across the table to each of Richelieu's neighbours, while pointedly ignoring the duke himself. Richelieu must by this time have known the Bourbons well enough to be beyond any possibility of surprise, but to a man so sensitive as he, even such petty discourtesy could hardly fail to be wounding. Though no doubt it did not strike so deeply as the violent attacks in the Chamber on his late ministry which were allowed to pass unchecked by Villèle, or the malicious exultation of the royalist press over " the fortunate ministerial revolution of the month of December."

At the beginning of May 1822, after having sat through a further round of embittered wrangling in the Chamber of Peers, Richelieu felt the need for another visit to Courteilles. The night before his departure from Paris he dined with Pasquier, who among his other guests had a certain Dr. Bally, just returned from Barcelona where yellow fever was then raging. The doctor and the duke spent an evening of absorbing interest comparing notes on their respective experiences in fighting yellow fever and plague, and on taking leave of Pasquier the duke departed in good spirits. The next day he set off for Courteilles, followed as usual by his " Madwoman of a Queen " who had not ceased her infatuated persecution of him. At Courteilles she took up her abode in a little inn just opposite the château, from which vantage point she could watch his comings and goings, to the helpless fury of her victim.

A few days after his arrival, having gone out riding according to his habit, Richelieu rode across a ford which turned out to be deeper than he had expected. But with his usual indifference to matters of dress, he did not trouble to change his wet clothes when he returned to the château. As a result of this carelessness, he developed a severe feverish chill, and since he evidently felt no confidence in the local doctor whom the duchess was anxious to call in, he decided to return to Paris, writing to Roger de Damas that when he arrived back there he must clearly put himself in the hands of the doctors. But as he entered his carriage to leave Courteilles, those standing by were shocked to see how ill he looked and before the journey had progressed very far, the aide-de-camp who was travelling with him was alarmed to observe undoubted signs that the duke's fever was increasing. At Dreux, where they stopped to change horses, the Queen of Sweden overtook them, and at once had her carriage drawn forward so that she might gaze on her duke while he was helplessly immobilised. But it did not need the eye of adoration to tell her that the man whom she saw inside the other carriage was very far from well, and in great agitation she summoned the aide-de-camp and said to him : " Sir, you must take the responsibility of having the Duc de Richelieu bled upon the spot." The aide-de-camp, however, obviously decided that he would do nothing of the kind, not even on receiving repeated instructions to the same effect at Pontchartrain and again at Versailles, and although, as her agitated Majesty of Sweden pointed out, the duke was so ill that he had not even troubled to pull down his carriage blind on the side where she was standing.

They reached Paris on the afternoon of the 22nd May, by which time the duke's condition was evidently showing some improvement, since he went as usual to visit Mme de Montcalm. But he was unable to eat much of the food she offered him, and on returning to his house, Léon de Rochechouart took charge of him and induced him to send for the doctor. By a most unfortunate chance, however, Richelieu's usual doctor, Bourdois, was himself ill, and had to send a substitute, Lerminier, who knew nothing of the patient, but had been warned that he was very highly-strung and that his health was therefore closely affected by his nerves. Richelieu, as can be imagined, did not view the appearance of a complete stranger at such a moment with the least enthusiasm and rejected on the

spot various remedies which he proposed. Lerminier therefore confined himself to prescribing an infusion of orange
leaves and said that he would return the following day. He
then reported the result of his visit to Bourdois, who said that
the duke was always irritable and difficult when he had a little
fever.

But soon after the doctor's departure, Richelieu had a
stroke. The Abbé Nicolle who came in to visit him, found
the duke unable to utter a word ; he could only press his old
friend's hand, while a few tears trickled slowly down his
cheeks. The Abbé Feutrier of the Church of the Assumption
was called to administer the last rites, and the duke appeared to
be able in some degree to follow the prayers which were being
recited for him at his bedside. But as the day drew to a close he
lapsed into complete unconsciousness and at about eleven p.m.
he quietly passed away. The Marquis de Castelnau, having
heard that the duke was ill, but not knowing of his serious
condition, hurried to visit him and was horrified on reaching
the house to be met with the news that Richelieu was dead.

Before his interment in the Church of the Sorbonne, the
duke's body was temporarily laid in the Church of the Assumption. Here his poor " Madwoman of a Queen " came to take
her last farewell of him, hiring a pew where, says Mme de
Boigne, " she spent days and nights in unrestrained grief " ;
after which, nothing remained for her but to return to her
long-suffering spouse in Sweden. Before Richelieu's body
was transferred to the Sorbonne, his widow expressed the
wish to have his heart, and this was duly carried to her in a
lead casket by the Abbé Nicolle, escorted by the two cousins,
Rochechouart and Rastignac. It was placed in the chapel wall
of the château at Courteilles, and when the duchess herself
died in 1830, the casket was transferred to her tomb. In the
Church of the Sorbonne, where its builder, Cardinal Richelieu,
lies in a finely sculptured tomb of Carrara marble facing the
principal door, a monument was erected to the memory of the
fifth duke close to the street door of the church. It is also of
white marble, but from France, not Italy, and along its base it

bears the significant inscription : " To the Duc de Richelieu, who preserved for France the Rhine frontier."

Yet even after his death, Richelieu did not cease to be the target of Ultra spite. Though the large crowd present at his funeral was drawn from all walks of life and included the entire diplomatic corps, there was no representative of the royal family present, nor indeed any of Monsieur's set. The Grand Almoner refused to officiate at the funeral because, he said, he could not officiate outside his diocese ; yet strange to say, this had not prevented him a few days earlier from consecrating a chapel for Mme du Cayla at the château of St. Ouen which had been bestowed on her by the old King. When Pasquier, as was only fitting, wished to send to the official government organ, the *Moniteur*, a short tribute to his old chief, and in accordance with the new Press regulations submitted it first to the cabinet, they did not hesitate to suppress its publication. Yet even Talleyrand, who could scarcely be described as Richelieu's friend, made the famous remark " He was some-body," and said of him that " his was one of those great lives which only this time and rare circumstances can create ; such lives are only replaced with the utmost difficulty and it is a calamity when they disappear from a country."

There was, however, one part of the world at least where Richelieu was neither unappreciated nor forgotten : the pro-vinces of New-Russia, and above all, the town of Odessa, where on receipt of the news of his death a state of general mourning was declared and all public entertainments closed down. A subscription was opened to collect funds for the erection of a statue and this was unveiled in May 1828. It was in bronze, since marble was considered unsuitable to the climate, and it bore round its base three bas-reliefs representing agriculture, commerce and justice. Above them stood the figure of Richelieu with his right hand stretched out, as if pointing out to Russia the buildings which he had raised, the harbour which he had filled with ships, the highways he had opened to the Mediterranean and the East. The inscription stated that the statue was erected by the grateful people of the three governments of Ekaterinoslav, Kherson and the Crimea, to the memory of their Governor who had laid the foundations of Odessa's prosperity.

But no one indeed mourned more sincerely for Richelieu than the Tsar. Like Richelieu, he had been called upon to occupy a position for which he felt himself to be utterly unfitted ; his efforts to lead Russia along the path of enlightened reform had brought him only frustration and bitter disillusionment, while his projected Holy Alliance, described by the hardened realist Castlereagh as " a piece of sublime mysticism and nonsense," was in the eyes of his European colleagues merely evidence of a deranged mind. (" It was not without difficulty that we went through the interview with becoming gravity," wrote the British Foreign Secretary to his government after the Tsar had unfolded his proposal to Castlereagh and Wellington.) Alexander's reign was now drawing towards an end as enigmatic as his own personality, and he told La Ferronays : " I weep for the Duc de Richelieu as the one friend who made me understand the truth. He was the very model of honour and loyalty. The services he has rendered me in Russia will for ever claim the gratitude of every honest man. I mourn for him also on behalf of the King, who will find in no one else such disinterested devotion. I mourn for him on behalf of France, where he was poorly appreciated and to whom, nevertheless, he rendered such great services."

Yet among Richelieu's own countrymen, it was strangely enough one of the royal princes who pronounced what was perhaps a most fitting epitaph. Alone among members of the royal family in expressing regret at Richelieu's death, the Duc d'Angoulême had both the courage and the honesty to say of him : " He did not like us, but he loved France."

GENERAL

DONATION DU DUC DE RICHELIEU, in the Bibliothèque Victor Cousin at the Sorbonne.

This large bequest of manuscript material from the archives of the Richelieu family, presented to the University of Paris by the Duc de Richelieu before the last war, contains forty-three volumes (Nos. 68–110) dealing with the fifth duke, including, besides journals, correspondence, documents, etc., one devoted entirely to biographical accounts of him written by his wife, Langeron, Sicard and Lainé. The contents of this volume have been published, together with some of his Russian and French correspondence in the *Recueil de la Société Impériale russe d'Histoire*, LIV (St. Petersburg, 1886), which is thus the most extensive printed source of first-hand biographical material.

(Other portions of this bequest, such as the Journal of the Marquise de Montcalm and Richelieu's letters to the Marquis d'Osmond, have also been published by the late M. Sébastien Charléty : see below.)

Rochechouart, Comte Léon de. *Souvenirs*. Paris. 1889.

As Rochechouart was not only Richelieu's cousin and second aide-de-camp, but had charge of the duke's household in Odessa and Paris, his memoirs are of considerable interest as a first-hand account of Richelieu's life and personality.

Boigne, Ctsse. de. *Mémoires*, II, III. Paris. 1907.

Entertaining, but sometimes spiteful, and not always accurate in facts or dates. (But the latter is a common failing in memoirs of this period, which were usually written in the old age of their authors, many years after the events described.)

Crousaz-Crétet, L. de. *Le duc de Richelieu*. Paris. 1897.

The only complete and fully documented account of Richelieu's career which has appeared in France.

PART I

Family, etc. :
Batiffol, L. *Autour de Richelieu*. Paris. 1937.
Bossebœuf, L. A. *Histoire de Richelieu et ses environs*. Tours. 1890.

Cramail, A. de. *Le château de Richelieu.* Fontainebleau. 1888.

Ducros, L. *French Society in the Eighteenth Century.* London. 1926.

Hanotaux, G. *Histoire du Cardinal de Richelieu,* I. Paris. 1932.

Perkins, J. B. *Richelieu.* London. 1900.

Veuclin, V.E. *Les dernières châtelaines de Courteilles.* Verneuil. 1901.

Williams, H. N. *The fascinating Duc de Richelieu.* London. 1910.

Early years :

Asfeld (d'). *Voyage du duc de Richelieu.* Paris. 1827.

Damas, Cte. Roger de. *Mémoires,* I. Paris. 1912.

Wassiltchikoff, A. *Les Razoumowski,* II. Part IV. French ed. A. Brückner. Halle. 1894. (Correspondence of Count Andrew Razumovski with Langeron.)

PART II

Archives du Ministère des Affaires Etrangères :

Correspondance politique : Russie, XXVI. Mémoire sur la Russie. (Leclerc.)

CLI. Mure, Fr. consul at Odessa, to Caulaincourt.

Caulaincourt to Champigny.

Mémoires et Documents : XX, XXIII. Mémoires inédits du Comte de Langeron.

Castelnau, Marquis de. *Essai sur l'histoire de la Nouvelle-Russie.* 3 vols. Paris. 1827.

Frappaz, Abbé. *Vie de l'abbé Nicolle.* Paris. 1857. (Contains Richelieu correspondence.)

Pingaud, L. *Le duc de Richelieu en Russie.* Paris. 1882.

Pingaud, L. *Les Francais en Russie et les Russes en France.* Paris. 1886.

PART III

Archives du Ministère des Affaires Étrangères :

Correspondance politique : Angleterre 607, 609, 614.

Autriche 397–9.

Russie 156–8, 161–2.

Mémoires et Documents : 694–8, 700–14 (Peace settlement).

716–20. (Troppau and Laibach).

Bibliothèque Nationale :
MSS. français. 20280. Nouvelles Acquisitions :
Correspondance du duc de Richelieu au duc Decazes, 1815–17.
British Diplomacy, 1813–15. (Ed. C. K. Webster). London. 1921.
Correspondance diplomatique des ambassadeurs et ministres de Russie en France et de France en Russie avec leur gouvernements, 1814–20. A. Polovtsoff (publisher). Ed. de la Société Impériale russe d'Histoire. 3 vols. St. Petersburg. 1901–7.
Broglie, Duc de. *Souvenirs*, II. Paris. 1886.
Chateaubriand. *Mémoires d'outre-tombe*, IV. Paris. 1849–50.
Chateaubriand, Mme de. *Les Cahiers*. Paris, 1909.
Cisternes, R. de. *Le duc de Richelieu*. Paris. 1898. (Contains Richelieu's correspondence with Louis XVIII from Aix, and his memoir " Ma retraite du pouvoir.")
Daudet, E. *Louis XVIII et le duc Decazes*. Paris. 1899.
Fouques-Duparc, J. *Le troisième Richelieu*. Lyon. 1952. (Deals mainly with the peace settlement and liberation of the territory, but also contains Richelieu's journal of the Hundred Days, and a useful list of sources.)
Guizot, F. *Mémoires pour servir è l'histoire de mon temps*! I, II. Paris. 1858.
Metternich. *Mémoires*! III, IV. Paris. 1881.
Molé, Comte. *Mémoires*, II–IV. Paris. 1923–4.
[1] Montcalm, Marquise de. *Mon çournal pendant le premier ministère de mon frère*. (Ed. S. Charléty.) Paris. 1935.
Nettement, A. *Histoire de la Restauration*, V. Paris. 1860.
Pasquier, Baron. *Mémoires*, III–V. Paris. 1890.
Rougé, Cte. de. *Le Marquis de Vérac et ses amis*. Paris. 1890. (Letters from Richelieu during his tour of the Midi in 1819.)
[1] Richelieu, Duc de. *Lettres au Marquis d'Osmond*, 1816–18. (Ed. S. Charléty). Paris. 1939.
Serre, Cte .de. *Correspondance*, II–IV. Paris. 1876–77.
Talleyrand. *Mémoires*, III. Paris. 1891.
Vaulabelle. *Histoire des deux Restaurations*, IV–VI. Paris. 1857.
Viel Castel. *Histoire de la Restauration*, IV–X. Paris. 1860–
Villèle. *Mémoires et correspondance*, I, II. Paris. 1889.
Wellington. *Supplementary Despatches*, XI, XII. London. 1864.

---

[1] Published from MSS. in the Donation du Duc de Richelieu in the Sorbonne.

INDEX

AIX-LA-CHAPELLE, 31, 121, 160–5 (Congress), 168–9, 178.
ALEXANDER I, Tsar of Russia (1777–1825). Dislike of Talleyrand, 9; first meeting with R., 55; accession, 57; makes R. Governor of Odessa, 59, and Governor-General of New Russia, 75; war with Turkey, 85; alliance with Napoleon, 91–2; recalls R. from Odessa, 109; meets Mme de Krudener, 122–3; persuades R. to take office, 131; champions France over peace treaty, 142–4 and liquidations, 150; attitude over *Chambre introuvable*, 156–7; idea of a general alliance, 163–4; advises R. against retirement, 168–9; invites R. to revisit Russia 1819, 178–9; his attitude on R's second tenure of office, 194–5; on Spain, 199, and the Mediterranean, 201–2; his final tribute to R., 218.
ANAPA, 88–9, 93, 96.
ANGLÈS, Comte Jules (1778–1828), Prefect of Police, 204–5.
ANGOULÉME, Louis Antoine de Bourbon, Duc d' (1775–1844), 157, 185, 218.
ANGOULÉME, Marie-Thérèse Charlotte (Madame Royale), Duchesse d' (1778–1851), 117–18, 187, 214.
ARMANDINE, *see* MONTCALM, Marquise de.
ARTOIS, Charles-Philippe (Monsieur), Comte d' (1757–1836) 19, 117, 121, 130, 136–7 (his *gouvernement occulte*); sends Bruges to England, 154; the Secret Note, 160; his intrigues, 170; appeals to R. to take office again, 186–7; renewed intrigues, 204; R's final appeal, 209–10; continued ill-will to R., 213.

BENDER, 38, 47, 48, 87.
BERNADOTTE, Mme, *see* SWEDEN, Queen of.
BERRY, Charles Ferdinand d'Artois, Duc de (1778–1820), 121, 157, 185, 188, 191, 194.
BLACAS, Duc de (1770–1839), 117, 124–5, 126, 139, 197–8.
BOIGNE, Comtesse de (1781–1866). Née Charlotte d'Osmond, 24, 26–27, 114–16, 133, 135, 180–1, 183–4, 216.

BROGLIE, Duc de (1785–1870), 172–3.
BRUGES, Vicomte de (1764–1820), 154, 157–8.

CANNING, George (1770–1827), 158.
CAPODISTRIAS, Count John (1776–1831), 75, 144, 149, 166, 195, 196, 204.
CARAMAN, Vicomte de (1762–1839), French Ambassador to Vienna, 149, 195–6, 197.
CASTELNAU, Marquis de, 72, 80, 216.
CASTLEREAGH, Lord (1769–1822), British Foreign Secretary, 119, 122, 143, 144, 148, 149, 150, 156, 161, 162, 163–4, 195, 199.
CATHERINE II of Russia (1729–96), 29, 36, 39, 49, 51–2, 53, 54, 55–6.
CAYLA, Mme du, 209, 211, 217.
Chambre Introuvable, 128–9, 151, 155–7, 166.
CHARLES EDWARD, Prince (1720–88), the Young Pretender, 22.
CHATEAUBRIAND, Vicomte de (1768–1848), 9, 120, 134–5, 165.
CHINON, 15, Comte de, *see* RICHELIEU.
CIRCASSIANS, 65, 76–7, 88–9, 92, 95, 96–7.
CONDÉ, Prince de, 51.
CONSTANT, Benjamin (1767–1830), 116, 169.
CORBIÈRE, Comte de (1767–1853), 188, 190, 205–6, 209, 211.
CORVETTO, Comte (1756–1822), 139, 140, 150, 157, 173.
COURTEILLES, 27, 50, 52, 71, 114, 153, 177, 213, 214–5, 216.
COSSACKS, 65, 76–7, 88, 89–90, 92–3, 105.

DAMAS, Roger, Comte de (1765–1823), 28, 38, 42, 44, 46, 48, 215.
DECAZES, Élie, Duc (1780–1860), 24, 115–6, 135, 138–9, 140, 141, 156–7, 166, 167–72, 175–6, 182–3, 185–7, 190, 195, 206, 209.
DOCTRINAIRES, The, 138, 166, 167, 170, 178, 190–1.
DONNADIEU, General Vicomte (1777–1849), 155, 206.

EKATERINOSLAV, 65, 75, 78, 79.
ELECTIONS, 165, 166, 169, 203.

ELECTORAL LAW, The, 166, 170, 172, 173, 177, 178, 182, 189–90, 191.

FOUCHÉ, Joseph, Duc d'Otrante (1763–1820), 9, 115, 127, 129, 167.
FRONSAC, see RICHELIEU.

GERMAN COLONISTS in Russia, 65–6, 73.
GUIZOT, François (1787–1874), 138, 166, 190–1.

HARDENBERG, Prince von (1750–1822), Prussian Chancellor, 142, 149, 161.
HYDE DE NEUVILLE, Baron (1776–1857), 134, 155, 203.

ISMAIL, 36, 39–47, 86, 87–8.

JASSY, capital of Moldavia, 38, 48, 87.
JORDAN, Camille (1771–1821), 138, 191.
JOSEPH II, Austrian Emperor (1741–90), 23, 31, 55.
JUMILHAC, Simplicie, Comtesse de, 25, 57, 82, 133.
—— Odet de, 57, 175.

KHERSON, 65, 75, 78, 79, 95, 107.
KRUDENER, Julie de Wietinghof, Baronne de (1764–1824), 122–3, 143.
KURAKIN, Prince Alexis, 104–5, 107.

LAFAYETTE, Marquis de (1757–1834), 116, 117, 126, 169.
LA FERRONAYS, Comte de (1777–1842), French Ambassador in St. Petersburg, 92, 196–7, 198, 201, 218.
LAIBACH, Congress of, 197–9.
LAINÉ, Vicomte (1767–1835), 134, 140, 157, 166, 168, 170–2, 201, 206.
LANGERON, Andrault, Comte de (1763–1831), 23, 24, 37, 46, 51, 53, 54–5, 88, 113, 114, 128, 147, 152, 156.
LAWRENCE, Sir Thomas (1769–1830), 161–2.
LIGNE, Prince de (1735–1814), 23, 36.
LIGNE, Prince Charles de, 23, 36, 37, 41, 44–5, 46, 51–2.
LIVERPOOL, Lord (1770–1828), 118, 143, 164.
LOUIS XVIII (1755–1824), 55, 109, 113, 116, 117, 120–1, 123, 124, 125, 126, 129, 130, 139, 141, 143–4, 156–7, 164, 168, 170–2, 184, 185–6, 194, 195, 197, 208, 211.
LOUIS, Baron (1755–1837), 113, 139, 172, 183.

METTERNICH, Clement Wenceslas, Prince von (1773–1859), 33, 142, 149, 164, 195–8.
MOLÉ, Comte (1781–1855), 10, 135, 140, 141, 157, 170, 171, 173.
MONTCALM, Armandine, Marquise de (1777–1832), 25, 57, 81–2, 94–5, 96, 109, 114, 133–5, 145, 165, 176, 215.
MONTMORENCY, Mathieu, Vicomte de (1766–1826), 130–1, 185.
MOUNIER, Baron (1784–1843), 161, 188, 204.

NAPLES: Queen of, 105–6; marriage of princesses, 48; revolution, 192–200.
NAPOLEON (1769–1821), 59, 92, 98, 99, 113, 116, 119, 120, 125, 129, 140, 148.
NARISHKIN, Mme, 95–6, 98.
NEY, Marshal (1769–1815), 120, 136–7.
NEY, Mme, 118.
NICOLLE, Abbé (1758–1835), 27, 53, 70, 102, 103, 118, 131, 147–8, 168, 207, 216.

OSMOND, Marquis d' (1751–1838), French Ambassador in London, 148, 149, 150, 151, 156, 157.

PASQUIER, Etienne Denis, Baron (1767–1862), 134, 157, 170, 173, 185, 188–9, 190, 196, 197, 199, 201, 202, 205, 208, 210, 211, 217.
PAUL I, Tsar of Russia (1754–1801), 56–7, 67.
PIEDMONT, revolution in, 199–200.
PLESSIS, du, see RICHELIEU.
POIX, Prince de; Antoine Claude, Comte de Noailles (1777–1846), 21, 121.
POLIGNAC, Auguste Jules, Prince de (1780–1847), 130, 155, 187.
POTEMKIN, Prince (1736–91), 36, 38–9, 41, 48.
POZZO DI BORGO, Carlo Andrea, Count (1764–1842), 75, 134, 144, 147, 151, 155, 156, 158, 161, 171, 182, 194, 199.

RAZUMOVSKI, Count Andrew (1752–1836), Russian Ambassador in Vienna, 53, 54, 56.
RICHELIEU, Armand Jean du Plessis, Cardinal and first Duc de (1585–1642), 14–16, 216.
Armand Emmanuel Sophie Septimanie du Plessis (1766–1822), Comte de Chinon, 1766–88, Duc de Fronsac, 1788–91, then fifth Duc de Richelieu.
Birth, 19; education, 20–1; travels to Italy and Vienna, 22–3; appearance and character, 23–5; marriage, 22,

26–8 ; attends imperial coronation, 32–5 ; serves at Ismail, 37–49 ; mission to Condé, 51 ; proscribed as an *émigré*, 52 ; enters Russian service, 53–4 ; first meeting with Alexander, 55 ; resigns commission and goes to Poland, 56–7 ; recalled by Alexander, 57 ; revisits France, 57–8 ; made Governor of Odessa, 59 ; his work for the town, 69–73 ; made Governor-General of New-Russia, 75 ; reorganises Kuban Cossacks, 76–7 ; his life in Odessa, 79–83 ; captures Akerman on expedition against Turks, 85 ; expedition against Circassians, 88–9 ; provisions Moldavian army, 90 ; summoned to St. Petersburg for consultations with Tsar, 92 ; strange affair of War Ministry order, 93 ; expedition against Sudjuk-Kalé, 95–7 ; plague in Odessa, 100–5 ; R's spiritual awakening, 103 ; visit of Queen of Naples, 105–6 ; called to Vienna by Tsar, 109 ; returns to France, 109 ; follows princes to Ghent, 121 ; rejoins Tsar at Heidelberg, 123–5 ; returns to Paris after Waterloo, 127 ; persuaded to take office, 130–2 ; his attitude over Marshal Ney, 136–7 ; peace treaty negotiations, 142–5 ; liquidations, 146–51 ; evacuation of territory, 152–61 ; attends Congress of Aix-la-Chapelle, 161 ; resigns, 170 ; negotiations over Decazes, 171–2 ; proposed award to R., 174–5 ; made Master of the Royal Hunt, 175–6 ; tours the Midi, etc., 177–83 ; pursuit by Queen of Sweden, 180–4 ; appeals to R. to resume office after the murder of the Duc de Berry, 186–7 ; his second ministry, 188–9 ; his break with the Doctrinaires, 190–1 ; his views on French foreign policy, 193, 196, 201–2 ; Congress of Troppau, 195–7 ; Congress of Laibach, 197–9 ; renewed intrigues of Monsieur, 204–5 ; R. attacked in the address to the King, 208 ; his interview with the King, 208–9, and with Monsieur, 209–10 ; his resignation, 211 ; last illness and death, 214–16.
Louis Antoine Sophie du Plessis (1736–91), Duc de Fronsac till 1788 ; then 4th Duc de Richelieu, 19, 20–1, 29, 49.
Louis François Armand du Plessis, Marshal of France and third Duc de Richelieu (1694–1788), 16–19, 20–1, 28–9.

Rosalie de Rochechouart (1769–1830), Comtesse de Chinon, 1784–88, Duchesse de Fronsac, 1788–91, then Duchesse de Richelieu, 22, 26–8, 31, 50, 52, 57–9, 114, 177, 213, 215, 216.
ROCHECHOUART, Françoise de, 14.
ROCHECHOUART, Louis Victor Léon, General Comte de (1788–1845), 79, 80–1, 83–4, 89, 90, 91–5, 101, 103–4, 105, 106, 107–8, 109, 113, 114, 120–1, 126, 133, 178, 180, 181, 182, 215.
ROCHECHOUART, Rosalie de, *see* RICHELIEU above.
ROYER-COLLARD, Pierre Paul (1763–1845), 138, 157, 166, 190–1.

SECRET NOTE, The, 160.
SERRE, Comte de (1776–1824), 141, 172, 190–1.
SICARD, Charles, 68, 71–2, 82–3, 179, 211.
STAËL, Mme de (1766–1817), 116, 172.
STEMPKOWSKI, Colonel, 79, 84, 120, 176–7, 180.
STUART, Sir Charles (1779–1845), British Ambassador in Paris, 155–6.
SUVOROV, Alexandre-Vassilievitch, Count (1729–1800), 41–2, 43.
SWEDEN, Queen of (née Desirée Clary) (1770–1860), 180–4, 214, 215–16.

TALLEYRAND-PÉRIGORD, Charles Maurice de (1754–1838), Prince de Bénévent, 9–10, 125, 127, 129–30, 141, 167, 170, 171, 204–5, 206, 217.
TROPPAU, Congress of, 195–7.

URZUOV, 83–4, 179.

VÉRAC, Marquis de, 175, 177, 179, 182, 186.
VILLÈLE, Comte Jean de (1773–1854), 136, 171, 188, 190, 203, 205, 208, 209, 213, 214.
VITROLLES, Baron de (1774–1854), 129, 160.

WELLINGTON, Duke of (1769–1852). Invades S.W. France, 106 ; Ambassador in Paris in 1814, 118–19 ; in Brussels before Waterloo, 121 ; Waterloo and after, 125–6 ; his views on the peace settlement, 143, 144 ; the Ambassadors' Conference, 147 ; his financial arbitration, 150–1 ; the occupation, 153–6, 158 ; the *Chambre introuvable*, 157 ; attempted assassination, 159 ; at the Congress of Aix-la-Chapelle, 161 ; his gloomy prediction to R. over the freedom of the press, 169.